THE POWER OF MENTAL DISCIPLINE

A Practical Guide to Controlling Your Thoughts, Increasing Your Willpower
and Achieving More

Positive Psychology Coaching Series

IAN TUHOVSKY

Important

The book is not intended to provide medical advice or to take the place of medical advice and treatment from your personal physician. Readers are advised to consult their own doctors or other qualified health professionals regarding the treatment of medical conditions. The author shall not be held liable or responsible for any misunderstanding or misuse of the information contained in this book. The information is not indeed to diagnose, treat or cure any disease.

It's important to remember that the author of this book is not a doctor/therapist/medical professional. Only opinions based upon his own personal experiences or research are cited. The author does not offer medical advice or prescribe any treatments. For any health or medical issues – you should be talking to your doctor first.

I want to provide you with high quality, so if you think that one of my books/short reads can be improved in some way, please contact me at:

contact@mindfulnessforsuccess.com

I will be very happy to hear from you, because you are who I write my books for!

Contents

CHAPTER 1: THE POWER OF MENTAL DISCIPLINE

Mental discipline is one of those traits we hear a lot about. Go ahead and check out any motivational page on social media, any guide to gaining success/wealth/lovers, or any list to successful people and it'll come up almost every time. You'll see words like "work hard," "don't stop," and "believe in yourself". These are the actions you need to take, but they all stem from the same place. It's a place I've spent plenty of time working on in my own life after the people who mentored me drilled it into my psyche. Even now, I can remember the first time I heard the words clearly when one of those mentors – a former special forces operator – was being asked about the most important individual trait to possess in the special forces world.

"Self-Discipline"

Quite clear and concise, isn't it? But what does it mean? Well, the journalist wanted to know too, so the answer was explained. The exact words have been lost to time, but the message was simple; it's the ability to push yourself with no outside encouragement or instructions. It's the ability to persevere and believe when all else seems to be falling apart. It's the ability to stay positive and adapt in the face of challenges or to push yourself when nobody else is watching.

In a nutshell, discipline is the core trait behind those skills, which will make a difference in high-pressure situations. Special forces units are trained to deal with the most extreme high-pressure situations in the worst of settings. These soldiers could find themselves deep behind enemy lines when things go wrong, with almost no help of any type. They are specialists who can deal with these situations and *still* get the job done – no matter what goes wrong along the way.

What Mental Discipline Means

People will often ask a successful businessman or athlete how they manage to keep on driving through to achieve their goals. After all, we all *think* we want to live the lives of the super-rich. The truth is that most people are only looking at the rewards and not the work that goes into getting there.

Elon Musk is a great example of this. He's mega rich, being worth over $20 billion, and is known all over the world already thanks to his innovative creations. To top it off, his last few relationships have all been with young, super attractive actresses and singers. There are plenty of men out there who'd love to have these perks and many women who'd love the opposite too.

What they don't see is that Elon has always had an *insane* work ethic. He taught himself how to program a computer at age 10 and had sold his first program at 12. Read that again. He didn't only succeed as a programmer at age 12, but he *taught it to himself* in 2 years! He also overcame teen years full of relentless bullying, then left the country against his dad's wishes to start fresh in Canada – age 17.

The high-risk plays continued with several business launches, and Musk invested a ridiculous amount of hard work to get where he is today. Even now, 30 years later, he still keeps a busy schedule. Word is that he has cut back a little though, having "easier" 90-hour work weeks.

Imagine if you had $20 billion, 5 kids, and an insanely hot girlfriend to see – how tough would you find it to get out of bed and take on a 14-hour day early in the morning? Or to crank it up during important times and take to just sleeping in your office so *every moment was spent on work?*

What is it that keeps Elon Musk going day after day, instead of just riding into the sunset and enjoying his rewards?

It's discipline. That powerful, self-imposed trait of mental discipline is what keeps somebody like this going. It's what made Michael Jordan one of the greatest basketball players of all time when he continued the habit of constant practice from childhood into his late career. The Williams sisters also grew up living the sport of tennis day after day, before and after school, to become the dominant players they became.

All of this comes under the ability to motivate yourself, to discipline yourself into doing whatever is necessary. That might be long, hard practice in the times when nobody is watching. It may mean making your own plans and taking the chance without instruction from the outside. It can mean digging deep to endure any level of pain or hardship as you continue pushing through regardless - much like the soldier mentioned earlier would have done.

See, mental discipline is the underlying factor that fuels the traits of successful people. It's the reason they can endure, it's the driving force behind the desire to learn, it's the biggest reason why successful people will continue to work hard when they could just as easily quit and cash out.

EFFORT VERSUS TALENT

The biggest problem with many people today is that they believe success generally comes down to either luck or talent. It doesn't.

Firstly, luck is a random factor. Of course, there is going to be a very tiny minority who will actually succeed purely to luck. These are the lottery winners, the lucky gamblers, and the reality TV stars of the modern age. For most of these people, success will be fleeting. Lottery winners, for example, have a tendency to go broke. This is because they never learned the ability to handle money on the way to their riches, nor did they learn the value of the work that would go into it. Because of that, they tend to waste the cash and run out long before they should have. Other times it's lost by descendants, on poor ventures, or the cash simply runs out because there isn't an ability to earn more with it.

The effort and struggles, which so many successful people have been through, are character building experiences. They're the reason these people now have mental toughness, a sharp business mind, and the ability to take calculated risks. It's the reason they have the discipline to be smart with their money and also the reason they value their success. Those hard times, which had to be endured at some point, are all part of the real cost behind success.

Talent is similar. It can be spectacular. Many people out there have some level of talent, but it's hard work and discipline that are needed for success. Most athletes have a common theme of constant hard work from a very young age. This is what it takes to become an Olympian, a Hall of Famer, or a World Record holder.

A study by Stanford professor Carol Dweck explored the effects of talent versus effort in 1999. The study was created to explore what effects praise could have on children and their ability to perform academically. In the study, a random group of school children was divided in half and given an IQ test.

One group was then praised for their results by being told they must be *talented* or *smart* to achieve the scores they had. The other group was praised for their *hard work*, which, they were told, must have been the reason they achieved their scores.

After this, they were given the choice of taking a similarly difficult test or a tougher one. In the group praised for talent, the majority chose to take a similar test. The belief is that this relates to their perception of having achieved well because of innate talent. A harder test would, therefore, be harder to get the same score on.

Meanwhile, the second group almost entirely chose to take the more difficult test. Again, the hypothesis is that the belief in hard work drove these children to believe they could achieve more by attempting more difficult challenges.

It's pretty easy to see how something like this can relate to ambition and drive. A belief in hard work, in discipline and effort, is important if you want to fuel ambition. High achievers are almost never created without discipline and drive.

Breaking Barriers

Another way mental discipline is manifested into real-world success is through belief. There are lots of individuals who overcame extremely limiting circumstances to become some of the best in the world at what they do. Stephen Hawking is a good example. Here's an absolute genius, one of the smartest minds of our time, who also happened to be diagnosed with ALS at the age of 21. At the time, he was told he could expect to live another couple of years as his physical abilities would decline rapidly. Despite losing almost all ability to move or talk over the coming decades, Stephen survived for another 55 years and used his time to think deeply on matters of physics, creating a number of popular theories within the subject.

Could he have done this if he simply accepted defeat and lost the drive and discipline to continue? Unlikely. How about Roger Bannister, the first man to run a four-minute mile? For centuries it was considered impossible, but from a young age, Roger would insist he was going to accomplish it – and he did. In 1954 he broke the four-minute barrier for the first time ever. What stands out about this story isn't that Bannister managed to beat the time. It's that his record was broken a couple of months later and that a year later there were three people breaking the four-minute mark *in a single race!* In the modern day, it's not even considered that spectacular anymore.

Again, what was it that caused this? Did runners suddenly become better at around the same time? No, but their belief in achieving a fast mile definitely did. Their belief that four minutes was possible, was doable, and could even be beaten, was incredibly solid.

The effect of mental discipline works in the same way. It's having an unshakeable belief in the possibility of something, and in your ability to achieve it – but this time *before* the tangible results exist.

By creating a solid mental image and drilling the right beliefs into your mind, you can hone this level of discipline. You can use it as a weapon, as part of your toolkit for life, and towards achieving anything you have ever wanted.

Know this though – discipline is not an easy trait to master. It *is* a simple one because there isn't much complexity to it. What it does require is effort and consistency, day after day and moment after moment. Soon we will get to the process of creating and maintaining mental discipline, broken down for you into helpful and practical steps. But remember, this isn't a guide to fast success, because no such thing exists. For your part of the bargain, you'll need to put in the effort not only when you're motivated but also when you're tired or stressed – and I will teach you in this guide *how* to deal with stress, tiredness, and other issues. After all, nobody can be happy and motivated all the time, but to succeed, you need the ability to push through these difficulties. That's what mental discipline truly is.

CHAPTER 2: SELF BELIEF

The world is full of big, beautiful structures, some of which look like miracles of engineering in the way they're built. Creations like the Palm Islands in Dubai, or the Channel Tunnel, look miraculous because until they were created, most people wouldn't believe the ideas to be possible. This rings true for plenty of other structures as well – the Burj Khalifa, the Large Hadron Collider, International Space Station, and more.

Yet all of these creations start in similar ways – as an idea. Now it's probably not big news to you that people have ideas every day, all over the world. Some are good, some are bad, others are great, terrible, or anything in between. What matters most though isn't the idea, it's the action taken on that idea. Action is what bring things to life, it's what turns an idea from a possibility into reality.

With some ideas, it's easy to do this. If your idea is to buy product A and try to sell it to your friends, then that's a pretty simple idea to bring to life. It still takes action though, and many people just don't ever take the steps that are needed to bring their ideas to life – regardless of whether the idea is simple or not.

So what is it that allows some people to take the action needed and get their idea off the ground? Whether the idea sounds simple or complicated, the answer is the same. These people have **self-belief** and they believe in their ideas!

If you've got a simple idea that you really believe in, you'll take the action needed. Think about it. Imagine you've discovered a product that you just *know* people will love. You have a gut feeling, deep-seated belief that this is going to be hot and popular. So, you go ahead and stock up, maybe even create a brand or company to sell as, and begin looking for customers. Congratulations, you're now in business and taking action. Why? Well, I can tell you now it isn't because your idea was *good*, whatever that means. People who believe in an idea being good or bad are usually relying on luck. They're looking for an idea, and opportunity, which is a sure thing – and these don't exist.

When Bill Gates first created Windows, he didn't do it in a world that *wanted* his operating system. He did it in a world where most people didn't even know what an operating system could be, but he did it in the *belief* that his system would be needed and popular as times changed – and he was right.

When Steve Jobs created the first iPhone, he did it going against the trend of what phones were supposed to be at the time. He created a unique brand based on his *belief* that people would value his brand identity and his unique touch, and buy his products because of that.

Both Jobs and Gates were working based on their own ideas and their own information. Of course, they would have studied the marketplace first to create their ideas. They would, in fact, have studied it deeply enough to fuel their own belief in the products they were creating. Make no mistake though, it was this *belief* that fuelled them and led to the success of their ideas.

You see, all success starts with the belief – in the idea and in yourself. You can't push yourself to develop an idea, a business, or even your health and relationships if you don't believe you have the ability to accomplish what's in front of you. That's where it all starts. Even the Palm Islands and the Channel Tunnel had a first step, a first stone to be laid, or the first area to be dug out. Once a plan is in place, everything can be broken down into steps and the next task in front of you. Before you can complete that task though, you need to have an unshakeable belief in the worthiness of your idea and your ability to pull it off.

The Relationship Between Self-Belief and Confidence

Confidence is an area of self-improvement that people focus massively on – and with good reason. Who doesn't want to be more confident, right? More confidence means you're less afraid of failure, you're more willing to try new ideas, and that you work harder when you apply yourself. Sounds great, doesn't it? Who wouldn't want all of that?!

What I'm here to tell you is that confidence *isn't something you find!* It's something you create, something you build from within – and it starts with self-belief.

If you believe yourself to be a problem solver or a hard worker, you'll stick with things when they become difficult and try your best to find a way through. On the other hand, if you believe you don't try hard enough and don't have the ability to solve problems, then you're a lot more likely to give up in times of difficulty.

This carries through all areas of life. People who don't believe they're attractive tend to get less dating opportunities because the lack of belief prevents them from putting themselves out there. In social situations, it isn't a type of personality or interest that makes people popular, it's their confidence in themselves and their belief that they are interesting people. With the belief in place, people become more social and share their interests and opinions. A belief in their own ability to hold a good conversation leads to more, and deeper, conversations taking place. All of this then fuels the belief further, because it's proven to be true. This cycle continues and creates powerful confidence in the social area. The same works for other areas of life; self-belief gives you the confidence to give it your best instead of a weak, half-hearted effort.

On the flipside, imagine a person who doesn't believe in their social skills. This lack of belief leads to low confidence. With constant doubts on whether they'll be liked as a person, or whether they're interesting enough, these people avoid the risk of a bad interaction and hold themselves back. They don't really engage in conversations and they don't really open up about themselves.

Where does this lead? Well, how would you react to a quiet, moody looking stranger who doesn't try to interact with you? Let's say you take the chance and introduce yourself anyway. The person you're talking to responds but is very awkward about it and gives short answers with no real info. They're giving you no information, not really asking any questions, or not taking the convo any deeper – how likely are you to become friends? Not very, right? This is the effect of low confidence and a lack of self-belief.

The impact goes further too. For the person who is lacking belief, the interaction has just gone pretty badly. They're left feeling awkward and unsure, glad that the chat has already ended, and left with confirmation that they aren't likable or sociable. This reinforces the lack of belief and creates a negative spiral instead of the positive cycle that begins with self-belief.

A lot of the time when we look around us, the people who are successful or unsuccessful are created by these spirals, whether they're good or bad. There are so many successful people out there who had their self-belief protected and nurtured as children. Their personalities are formed in a way that supports an adventurous, confident lifestyle and gives them the tools and coping mechanisms needed to walk this kind of path. From a young age, they get in the habit of trying hard, believing in themselves, taking chances, and brushing off any failures. They may also learn from mistakes and make adaptations. Along the way, this habit of success and the habit of succeeding turn them into successful adults. For these people, life has always been about going after what you want, and they usually tend to find their way there.

On the other side, there are people who were never really taught these skills at a young age. Perhaps they also had a tougher upbringing than most, growing up in poor surroundings or coming from broken families. Some may even have been victims of abuse or neglect, leading to any number of mental or emotional issues. For these people, life has always been a painful experience, one where they need to worry most about their own safety and security.

With safety being the priority, these people are less likely to take risks or chances. They will stick to what is safe and secure, which is usually what they already know. This is how they've lived up until now, and this is the way they've been kept safe. From an evolutionary standpoint, it's a pretty good choice. Why take on a risk when you don't have to? The problem is these people can't tell the difference between a worthy risk, a *calculated risk*, and a genuine life-changing risk. To a person with no self-belief, anything could be devastating to their life or their psyche.

The difference between self-belief and confidence is the effect it has and the area it covers. With **confidence**, we're usually talking about a specific area or skill. You might be confident that you're good looking but not in other areas. Somebody else might be confident in their math skills but not their social ability. Confidence tends to be attached to a category and can often be supported with actual proof. The confident mathematician has probably solved loads of math problems before, so there's definite, indisputable proof that they're good at math. This is why they have confidence.

When it comes to **self-belief**, we're usually talking in a more general way. If you believe in yourself strongly, you're probably willing to try anything, even if it's something you're not usually good at or a completely new skill. People with self-belief don't need proof of their skill level. They will happily believe in their own ability, or at least their ability to learn/improve, and will give most things a try.

I can tell you right now that confidence without self-belief isn't worth much. A person who's confident in their ability but lacks self-belief can be limited quite easily. Remember that confidence comes from the ability to perform in that area – this is what proves their ability and gives them confidence. Now imagine we have a good mathematician, one who is confident in their talents but who also lacks self-belief. Give them math problems that are at or below their current skill level and they will solve them easily. Give them tasks a little above their level, and they'll put a good effort in, trying to figure out or learn whatever is needed to solve the problem. However, give them a bunch of tasks that are quite hard at their current level, and they often begin to struggle.

With tough questions, wrong answers, and a lot of learning needed, confidence starts to wear away. Now the mathematician will begin to struggle a little, and as that happens, they'll begin to doubt themselves and their own ability. Confidence is shaken and they perform worse and worse over time. Looking at this situation makes it easy to see why confidence alone isn't good enough for long-term success. Confidence keeps you limited to the areas you're already good in and also to the level you're already performing at. From there, any steps up need to be small and gradual.

Compare this to a mathematician with self-belief, one who believes they can learn anything and reach any level, who knows that it just takes hard work and learning to get there. This mathematician might be more limited at the start because they don't have the specific math talent of the first guy. Thanks to their self-belief though, they will give a consistent effort and feel comfortable learning new things. In fact, they usually *want* to learn new things because they *believe* they are capable of more! This mathematician is potentially limitless – they will continue to develop until they hit the limit of their natural ability.

Confidence is limited to its own area. It doesn't give you self-belief. Self-belief is a general trait though; it affects your entire personality and every part of who you are. It can also give you confidence in specific areas.

BUILDING SELF-BELIEF

You've probably heard of people "being driven" before. I don't mean chauffeured around in a car, I'm talking about those people who just seem relentless in their pursuit. People like Elon Musk or Michael Jordan, people who won't stop until they win. Michael Jordan even wrote a book called *Driven From Within*, showing how important he considers it. If one of the greatest athletes of all time ranks drive so highly, it's got to be important.

Look at the name of his book again. What gives him his drive? Well, it comes "from within;" we know that much. Shall I tell you how he manages to power such an incredible drive? The fuel comes from his *self-belief*. MJ believes in himself so much he believes that he can do anything. As he says:

> *"I've always believed that if you put the work in, the results will come."*

It's quite clear to see how much he believes in himself. Looking past that though, he's clearly not talking about himself as something different, he's talking about *everyone*. MJ himself has admitted that we all have limits, but while most people use limits to explain their bad situations away, MJ *knows* you can succeed in most areas if you try hard enough. This is the first stone of self-belief, to know that you *can* succeed. *You* can succeed because *others* have succeeded, and most humans have quite a similar potential.

Could you be a NBA star? Highly unlikely at this point, *but* if you had been driven enough to spend your *life* practicing from when you could walk, then you could have been. Maybe not with the freakish peak of a guy like MJ, and you'd need a little genetic help in the size department for basketball specifically, but if you could tick that box then with that same amount of work, turning pro could have been possible.

The Williams sisters would not have been superstars without their childhood of constant work. MJ would not have been a legend if he didn't grow up constantly working on his game either. These are the facts of life. It's no coincidence that almost every top achiever in every field has been working tirelessly towards that goal for a long, long time.

When you know you can succeed, it's time to actually put the work in. This is the second building block of self-belief. You put the time in and do it in an effective way. So many people are caught up in staying "busy" without focusing on the most important step in front of them. Smart action always beats learning and studying, so get active in your endeavors, whatever they are. If you want to eat healthier, start making small changes now. If you want to be fitter, start exercising. Once you start to do the actions, your belief also begins to grow and you become better.

One important point to mention here is **don't fear failure!** Once again, we go back to MJ:

"I can accept failure, everyone fails at something. But I can't accept not trying."

This is the mindset of a man who walked away from a successful 10 year NBA career, at the pinnacle of the game, to try his hand as a baseball player in the MLB. Jordan himself has mentioned missing thousands of shots in basketball too, losing hundreds of games, and missing a game-winning shot on dozens of occasions. Yet he's still remembered as the greatest of all time. Why? Because failure doesn't matter.

Failure is temporary. It's a learning experience. All that matters is if you can eventually win or not; it doesn't matter how many losses it takes to get there. If you are truly working hard and pushing yourself, you are going to fail sometimes. That's okay though. Everyone fails. What matters is that you don't get bitter and twisted, or discouraged.

Take the failure, see what you can learn from it – failure is a much better teacher than success. Analyze your results and how you arrived at them. Is there something you could have done differently that would have helped you to succeed? Did you do things that weren't necessary or didn't have an impact? Treat failure as a step on the path to success – you've found another way NOT to do it, so you are closer to finding the right way just by process of elimination. Remember, doing the same thing and expecting different results is foolishness! Don't ever do it!

Once you've learned as much as possible from each failure, apply it to your future approach. Make changes and adapt so you don't fail in the same way next time. This way, even if you *do* fail again, it will be in a different way and for different reasons. From here you can again learn and adapt. Keep tweaking in this way, keep on learning and applying effort, and it's just a matter of time until you succeed!

THE IMPORTANCE OF SELF-IMAGE

Okay, we've covered confidence, self-belief, and drive. Now let's talk about self-image. Self-image is the way you see yourself, how you think and feel about yourself. A lot of people overlook this area, but it's massively important if you want to create a certain lifestyle or build specific skills and habits.

Remember how people with low self-belief are always expecting negative outcomes and tend to act in ways that lead to those outcomes? Well, self-image works in a similar way. If you think of yourself as having negative traits like being lazy, incompetent, or unproductive, then you're more likely to act those ways. If you generally look at yourself as a hard worker, a talented and productive person, then you are more likely to behave in that way.

It isn't as simple as just believing it when you want to. Self-image has to be a constant and consistent creation. You need to believe it all the time, and that belief has to be backed up by actions. When you act in a way that matches your self-image, it begins to grow and gain strength.

This doesn't mean you have to be entirely disciplined or productive from the start. If that was the case, there wouldn't really be much point in us talking about self-image, because you'd already be perfectly disciplined and driven by the time you had mastered this area. The best thing about self-image is that you can actually build it by using small actions. For example, if you want the self-image of an active go-getter, a problem solver who gets things done and stays productive, then you can start by building a simple routine for yourself and sticking to it. Going to bed at a set time, being up at the same time every day, always getting yourself ready properly in the morning – getting clean, making sure you're dressed well and that you smell good. This applies even if you're staying in the house, because you're doing it to create a standard for yourself and a self-image.

Take it further by dealing with problems head-on whenever they come up and avoiding procrastination. Do any quick jobs or chores immediately. A good tip here is to use the "5-minute rule." If it takes five minutes or less to do, do NOT put it off. Get it done now, and it's one more task knocked off your list.

Live like this for even a week and you'll start to feel the change. When I first got into good habits, back in my university days, all I really did was fix my sleep schedule and start applying the 5-minute rule. Every day I would also make sure I looked and smelled nice every morning, even if I was just going to stay in my dorm and work on the laptop anyway. I didn't actually realize how big the effects were until a couple of weeks later when I fell asleep at my friends' place after a night out. When I woke up, I felt so low and grimy because I couldn't get ready properly – I had no clean clothes, no toothbrush, and no aftershave! While everybody else lazed around and stayed how they were, I had to get out of there immediately.

Once home, I got ready and felt instantly better. I got a couple of quick tasks done, too (because of the 5-minute rule), and then realized I was feeling fresh, energetic, and ready for the day. Meanwhile, my friends were still laying around. I got plenty done that morning, while they did next to nothing. The small habits and standards I had for myself in the morning had created a persona that stayed active every day and always got things done.

Over the next few weeks, I noticed I was taking charge more in group situations and that I was more proactive about my own learning and work. From here, I started to fill my spare time with other productive activities and began my transformation into the successful business consultant and coach I have now become. It's always difficult to pinpoint when somebody becomes successful, but I know that for me, it all began with self-image.

Using self-image in this way allows you to choose who you want to be. You can set your own standards, depending on what you want to achieve, and build your image from there. What happened to me was that it created an "expected state," a certain way of living. My expected state is of a hard worker who always gets things done, no excuses. Tasks are handled head on and without hesitation, and I also hold myself to a high standard in terms of looks and my social life. Now if I behave in a way that goes against this, it causes a problem. Even if I just don't take the actions I'm supposed to, it feels uncomfortable. My mind and inner-self expect me to act in a way that matches my image and expected state, so that's where my thoughts and actions are naturally directed – I behave in a disciplined way without the discomfort of being disciplined. For me now, acting in an undisciplined way actually feels more uncomfortable!

Using self-image like this is another way to fuel your drive too. The self-image of a relentless worker who stops at nothing is only going to be sustained if you prove it with regular effort. Over time, that proof fuels the image – and the image then gives you more willpower, more drive, and more ability to dig deep – which fuels the image even more. It's a positive cycle and one you should be using to get ahead.

Chapter 3: Self-Belief and Weakness

A few years back I worked with a group of businessmen from Eastern Europe. They were an interesting mix of characters, similar in age and from differing backgrounds. The CEO had briefed me beforehand that there were a few standout performers in the group and had asked if there was some way to identify the traits these guys had, so we could focus on teaching them to the others.

Psychology has taught me there are usually only a few underlying options that people use to deal with most situations. I tried to find theirs by asking specific questions relating to their past performances and how they had succeeded. What I noticed was that all of them would mention consistent effort and **identifying what needed tweaking** or changing.

Having all the drive in the world is great, and it will probably see you succeed. You can be much more efficient if you target that drive into the right places though.

Identifying Weaknesses

Identifying a weakness can be tough for some people because their ego is fragile. That's what happens if self-belief is low, so you always need to start with your self-belief and creating that positive self-image. It still feels uncomfortable for most people to really analyze themselves and give an honest assessment, but it gets easier with time. Identifying weakness isn't just about seeing how you can change your sales tactics or adapt a business plan, it's also about tweaking yourself in general – the way you live, how you behave, your own knowledge and skills.

The most successful people in the world are able to identify areas for improvement in themselves and their businesses. This is what we need to do when it comes to discipline as well. We need to take an honest look back and see where we are missing the mark. Try to isolate the true cause of the problem. I found I used to procrastinate more and have less output when tired. The tiredness was a result of late nights, which was a result of getting up too late and having a slow start. Changing my morning routine to start earlier and be more efficient was tough at first. The earlier starts helped my output, but I wasn't really any quicker. Then I adapted and started falling asleep earlier with no problems. Now I was fully rested on my early starts and able to really crank up the work-rate.

So many people struggle with procrastination, it's no rare thing. There are plenty of superstar high achievers who still struggle with it too. The key is that you get a handle on it. For some people, they just need better rest, others need to be more organized and create a schedule, and there are people who benefit from dietary changes too. Stress management can be another idea to create a better and more productive mindset. For me, mindfulness and meditation are hugely beneficial in these areas.

The physical changes brought on by meditation have already been proven by science. Meditation has been shown to reduce a variety of illnesses and stress levels while improving focus and concentration. This is perfect for when you're trying to be more disciplined because you need to stay on point if you want to make progress.

Mindfulness is a similar practice but as a more general life approach. It really helps with fighting off impulsive thoughts and desires and makes your life more planned and stable. I've already written a fair bit about both of these in my other books so check those out if you're interested in learning more.

Getting back to our topic of weakness, you need to identify the issue and then come up with a way to solve it. Do this with one problem at a time, starting with the biggest, and you'll start to see how your life can change.

It also applies to your personality and how you deal with people. Thinking critically about your interactions can help you to shape your own persona. Being able to do this is almost like playing God in an RPG – you're creating a character with the stats you want. It's perfect for the business world because you can be perceived however you want. Create a persona and live it.

Some of you may have heard of NLP. It stands for Neuro-Linguistic Programming and is a psychological approach to changing your own sub-conscious. The theory is that your conscious brain is what you actively control, while your sub-conscious brain acts more instinctively. Using the right techniques, you can communicate with your subconscious and change it. It uses an approach where your language, thought, and behavioral patterns are modified. By behaving in a certain way, you trigger internal changes to mirror that mindset/approach.

Changing your behavior to improve on your weak points follows a similar method. You make the changes based on how you want to be performing. You can change social skills in this way. Let's pretend you want to improve your conversational skills because you don't feel like you really get out there enough. A good approach is to practice conversation as much as possible. Just start talking to people no matter where you are. Over time, all of the extra experience will make you much better at holding interesting conversations.

You can also study how to be better as you try this out, creating a smart two-level approach. You'll be studying what should work and trialing it in real-life too. Figuring out what works and dropping what doesn't, you could be a silver-tongued story-teller in no time at all.

When it comes to discipline, changes can be linked more to getting out of comfort zones or sticking to a game plan. For comfort zones, you can push yourself out in other areas to create a natural tendency towards it. Exercise really hard, take cold showers, do uncomfortable tasks. All of this will help you get out of your comfort zone in business and other areas of life too. Using routines and sticking to them, even minor things like a night-time stretching session, will help you to become more disciplined overall. Forging habits like this is important. There's one habit though that starts off as important, then becomes even more so over time. What is it?

Self-control.

SELF-CONTROL

Self-control is an essential piece of daily discipline. Without it, you're going to fall off pretty soon. To quote Jocko Willink, commander of SEAL Team 3's "Task Unit Bruiser:"

"That nice soft pillow, the warm blanket, nobody wants to leave that comfort – but you have to if you want to get a head start on everyone else."

Task Unit Bruiser contained "American Sniper" Chris Kyle, amongst others, all of whom saw heavy combat in Iraq. Willink was a decorated SEAL officer for 20 years and has always pushed discipline as his key to success. "Discipline Equals Freedom" is even the name of his second book.

Jocko pushes a number of simple approaches, which help you to control your life. Things like working from a to-do list or having a list of tasks prepared for the next day, so you don't really need to think too hard.

The reason self-control becomes more important over time is that some people start to slack off when good results start appearing. These results are encouraging, and people get over-confident and believe they're already there. Even I have suffered from this before. Throughout university and high school, I occasionally tried my hand at side businesses for a little extra income. These weren't big, impressive creations, just simple operations done locally.

With most of them I actually succeeded. Thing is, once I had enough cash to get by, I slacked off and eventually each venture died a slow death. I could have accelerated and made much more cash if I'd stayed hungry, but my own success was my downfall. I didn't have the self-control to resist temptation – nights out, late starts, and days off at all sorts of times. It's easy to see why I began losing business.

With self-belief and a smart approach to dealing with weak points, you're already quite well equipped to succeed. The next biggest hurdle is usually self-control. This is where discipline helps because you just need to stick with those routines and the steps you usually undertake.

Control also extends beyond your actions. It goes to your thoughts and emotions as well. Linking back to NLP, if you can get control over your own thought process, you can create the type of person you want to be. Gaining control of thoughts goes back to mindfulness as well. To go over it briefly, mindfulness makes you more aware of your thoughts as they occur and also more detached from them. This way you can observe them and discard them if not needed. Combine this with actively generating positive thoughts to create the mental state you want. It isn't easy, even though it sounds simple, because we all tend to have a lot of random, uncontrolled thoughts. Over time, we can still shape the way our brains work with persistent effort.

Emotional control allows you to better respond to situations. The man who comes to mind here is David Goggins, ultra-endurance athlete and former Navy SEAL, U.S. Ranger, and Paratrooper. This guy is a serious machine, and part of his approach is to constantly be outside of his comfort zones. Why? So he knows what pain feels like, he knows discomfort and stress, he knows what it's like to be hurt.

Having lived an extraordinarily tough life, this man has turned himself into somebody who can't be affected emotionally - he won't allow it. Sure, he feels like anybody else – but in the moment, he's able to shut that down, ignore the emotional side, and act rationally. Goggins had a tough childhood, growing up as the only black kid in a KKK dominated area. He endured plenty of racism and bullying. As an adult, he pushed himself to the extremes. This is a man who ran an ultra-marathon with NO training, completing the last 30 miles with fractures in his feet and legs. He also once held the 24-hour pull-up record – and tore tendons in his arms and hands on two failed attempts before achieving it. This is a man who now willingly goes towards hardship, because of what that discipline and drive gives back to him.

This is really important if you want to succeed in life, because sometimes things will go wrong. When they do, acting emotionally won't help. By mastering control over your emotional side, you can choose the best responses. You can also avoid being controlled by emotional manipulation. Control over your feelings helps with pushing through difficulty, handling setbacks, and even with generally maintaining a consistent effort. It removes the need for reassurance or positive feedback and allows you to operate without either – just like Navy SEALS such as Willink and Goggins had to.

CHAPTER 4: MENTAL TOUGHNESS

Having drive and direction is a great thing, but they won't last without another attribute – mental toughness. Mental toughness is defined as the ability to persevere through bad circumstances. Those "bad circumstances" could be anything at all, from an injury to bad weather to a generally hard situation. Sometimes it doesn't even have to be something particularly bad, it can just be a sudden and unexpected change. Any time we experience adversity, mental toughness is needed and can be a great help.

The power of the mind is an amazing thing, as we talked about in Chapter 1 when we covered Gates, Bannister, and four-minute miles. Belief can fuel you to reach your targets, and smart direction can get you there quicker. Toughness is different. Toughness isn't a fuel, it's a defender, which keeps you safe from the opposition attacks. Toughness is what you need when you're chasing that four-minute mile and begin to feel tired, out of breath, with burning legs and lungs, your mind telling you that you've done enough and it's time to stop. This is where toughness kicks in to keep you going at full speed, ignoring the negative signs and sticking to your guns.

The best time I saw this in action was during a military-run training camp. The participants in this session had done fitness testing a couple of weeks before. I had the results in front of me on a clipboard, so I knew which people were the strongest and fittest. I also knew that this camp would push them all physically, so they would all be tired, and that it would be the mental tests that really made a difference.

An early session involved getting everybody nice and tired with a couple of circuits and a quick run. From here, the group was made to do bodyweight exercises as a single unit, matching each other rep for rep. We told them we wouldn't stop until the five weakest people (out of 15) had quit. Now looking at the sheets, the five who quit first should have been the five who were weakest in testing. This didn't happen though. Instead, the five who quit were a mix from the lower to the upper-middle of the group. While these five weren't the physically weakest, they were the mentally weakest. I talked to a couple of them afterwards. Their reason for quitting?

"It was too much, I couldn't keep up with the rest."

"I'm just not as strong as the others, it's not my specialty."

"I tried my best, but it was just too much for me."

Do you notice how self-focused these reasons are? In some ways they look like a lack of self-belief, but belief was high at the beginning of the exercise. It's toughness that lacks, and it shows. When things get difficult, that's when toughness matters. It's like a nightclub bouncer when doubt tries to creep in. Toughness blocks it off and backs it down, keeping comparisons and thoughts of weakness out of your mind. A strong mind like this doesn't compare itself to others, it doesn't consider the end of the task or how well you're dealing with the situation. It keeps your focus single-minded on the task in front of you, and your own internal ability to keep pushing – even if it's only for one more rep. It lives in the now and only cares about what is happening this second. There isn't much thought or emotion involved, just action.

This mindset is exactly what allows a physically weaker person to outwork a stronger one. By taking each task, each exercise, and even each rep as a separate challenge, the mentally tough person is able to push through a lot more. It was shown during our tests when I questioned some of the weaker participants and asked how they were able to do so well. Here were some of the answers:

"I just focused on the next rep and nothing else."

"There was no way I was stopping unless I physically couldn't complete the exercise. Even though I did some bad reps, I was still moving."

"There was still some left in the tank, no point in stopping until it's empty."

As you can see, these people were focused only on themselves and only on what was immediately in front of them. For some of them, each rep was its own challenge – can I do it, or not? Breaking a tough task down like this is a popular way to get through it. The technique is known as "chunking" and is something we will look at more deeply in Part Two. It involves taking a long or difficult task and breaking it down into small chunk or stages. You can do this with overall plans or with tough events; you can even break it down to individual reps or ten seconds at a time. Now all you have to do is deal with the small chunk in front of you, which is actually a lot easier than it sounds. A lot of people don't believe they can do 100 press ups, but most of them will keep trying to do one press up again and again, potentially even passing 100 as they do.

Why does this work? Because when you are comparing yourself to the others, you only see the outside. You are seeing them complete an exercise but not hearing their self-doubt, aren't feeling their pain and tiredness, nor how close they are to quitting. From the outside, people look a lot stronger than they usually are (as long as they aren't voicing any complaints or discomfort).

Compare this with your own experience, where you *feel* all of the pain, tiredness, and doubt. You know each rep hurts, but when you watch somebody else you forget that. It's easy to see why comparing your performance here is no good thing. When you compare yourself, you know your own pain but not what the other person is going through.

 The only way comparison can be turned to a positive is if you have enough drive to match the performance of others, but again this comes from an internal belief of being stronger. That belief originates in self-belief and drive, but it still takes mental toughness to avoid doubts and keep it active. All of this comes down to the same thing – forget everyone else and focus on giving your all for the next step/rep.

When you focus only on the task at hand, you remove the mental comparisons and games. There's no more looking around and thinking others are finding it easy, or feeling like you're struggling more than others. Instead of these opinions and emotional thoughts, you focus on your own physical ability. Can you hold the position for another couple of seconds? Do it then. Got one more rep in you? Get it out. A lot of people using this technique will think they're only capable of one or two more reps, just to go on and crank out 10 more before the body starts to fail physically.

There's also no pressure because you aren't looking at the finish line or the massive amount that must be completed. You're ignoring those entirely and looking at the "chunk" in front of you. Just deal with that chunk, that's all. Don't even worry about the end. By using this approach, when it's all said and done you will have either cleared all of the chunks and completed the task or cleared as many as possible and found your actual limit – your actual physical limit, not what your mind believes the limit is. If this happens and you still fail, don't be downhearted. Rest easy because you have accomplished something most people never will by hitting your potential, even if it's only this one time, and this failure will be a building block for greatness – which isn't a failure at all really.

DEALING WITH DOUBTERS AND FAILURES

Extreme mental toughness is essential if you want to succeed at the highest levels. The highest levels are the hardest levels, so situations will be constantly changing and full of challenges. At the highest levels, it isn't just self-doubt that can be a problem, but also other people and their doubts.

The biggest example of this is of parents and their children. I can't count how many times I've seen parents tell their little ones to be realistic with their goals – that being a pro athlete, musician, or movie star is too tough and that they should aim for a college education and regular job. Yet there are kids out there who grow up to be pro athletes, musicians, and movie stars, so it MUST be possible! Along the way, a lot of these people are told they won't succeed. What's the difference between the ones who do and the ones who don't? Mental toughness!

Taylor Swift is a perfect example of this. From a very young age she had dreamed of being a successful popstar, and her parents backed her from the start. Her own desire created the drive and self-belief, but it was fed and reinforced by her parents. They nurtured her mental toughness with their continued support through hard times and early failures. In the early days, Swift was told several times that she wasn't good enough to be a musician.

Regardless, she continued working on her craft and pushing to hone her skills. Today she's worth hundreds of millions of dollars and is one of the most marketable and recognisable faces in the world. There's nobody who can say she isn't exactly what she dreamed of being– a successful popstar.

How many other potential Taylor Swifts are out there today, working 9 to 5 jobs because they were told to be realistic at a young age? How many potential superstars who never really tried because they listened to the people who said they weren't good enough?

Sometimes in life you're going to be told that you aren't good enough or that you're trying to perform the impossible. This is normal if you have big goals, because other people will find those goals intimidating. When people believe something is out of their reach, they're likely to believe you can't reach it either. It's important to remember that their opinion means nothing in the grand scheme of things. Opinions are free, everybody has one, and most of them are pretty useless. Listen only to people who have knowledge or experience that can actually help you. Don't worry about naysayers, because you will encounter negativity at times on your journey. Mental toughness is about being able to ignore them, resist them. Over time you may even find yourself able to use this negativity as fuel.

If you do come across people with inside knowledge, pick their brains on how things work, how to reach what you want, and what it takes to hit that next level. Learn from their experiences and use the knowledge to build on their abilities. Don't ask for opinion, ask for practical advice and make sure you apply it. Successful people love to share their knowledge, and seeing you make good use of it is the best compliment you can give.

Failure is the other thing that can set you back. Like I said, Taylor Swift was knocked back more than a few times and told she wasn't good enough. Her reaction is the best one to use in the face of any failure – don't accept it as a long term thing, but learn from it in the present moment.

She adapted her approach and worked on her craft even more, until she finally got the acceptance that she wanted. This came in the form of a record deal and album sales. Failure doesn't have to be final unless you let it. Every time you fail, take it as a learning experience. In fact, in some ways it's a good thing to fail, because every failure is a learning opportunity, a chance to get better. If you take this approach to your own process, you will get stronger and more successful after every failure that happens on your journey. With this approach, you become smarter and stronger over time, so it's inevitable that your goals will one day be within reach.

There isn't an automatic boost from failure though. You still have to view each situation critically and figure out what can be learned. What could you have done differently to succeed? What areas can you work on for next time? What skills do you need to develop? Remember that you need the ability to identify faults and weaknesses in order to grow. That's the real key to improving after failure.

CHAPTER 5: WILLPOWER

"The difference between a successful person and others is not a lack of strength, not a lack of knowledge, but rather a lack of will." – Vince Lombardi

"Willpower is the basis of perseverance." – Napoleon Hill

"Where there's a will, there's a way." – Anonymous

These are just a few of the thousands of quotes on willpower. It's always been a big theme in self-development. Plenty of successful people push it as one of the most important keys to how they did it.

So what is willpower? Put simply, it's the ability to control your own impulses. Do you have the ability to stick to a pre-made decision in the face of changing circumstances? This is what willpower is. It's being able to say no to food even when you're hungry because it hasn't reached your pre-set time to eat yet. It's getting up and hitting the gym when you already feel tired and it would be so much easier to just take one day off and rest...

You're probably familiar with willpower already, but what you might not know is that it's like any muscle in the body – it can be strengthened. Willpower is governed by the rational decision-making part of the brain, known as the prefrontal cortex. When you make impulsive decisions, what happens is the impulsive parts of your brain begin to literally overpower the prefrontal cortex. When you start to get impulsive thoughts and feelings it takes a strong amount of willpower to resist it. If the prefrontal cortex is strong enough, it can overpower these areas and shut them down, allowing you to stick to your original decisions. If it isn't strong enough though, your willpower will become overwhelmed and the impulsive desires will win.

Another similarity to physical muscle groups exists in how willpower can erode and shrink if it isn't used. Living without discipline and willpower can create bad habits. Keep in mind this doesn't mean you can't enjoy some time off here and there. The key is to implement some small habits into your routine that require willpower, and keep those constant. If you can stick to a couple of small willpower decisions in areas like wake up time, brief bouts of daily exercise, or eating healthily, then it's totally reasonable to enjoy your life in other areas – keeping moderation in mind of course! This means on vacation or special occasions, you can't just go crazy every weekend and expect to have good willpower after it. However, if you use a short morning routine with a few tasks to get done, and combine it with a small amount of daily exercise, wake up time, and a decent diet, then you can certainly enjoy most of your relaxation time without worrying about adverse effects.

Scientists have proven that the prefrontal cortex is involved in decision making and over-riding impulses. In lab studies, this is the area that lights up when decision making is involved, and it's the area that remains strong and in charge when people stick to their willpower. Impulse reactions cause activity in other parts of the brain, relating to the urges being felt at the time. Bad decisions occur when these areas become highly activated while the prefrontal cortex is worn down and can't match their activity level. This is what happens physiologically inside your brain when an impulse decision is made.

The good news is that science has also proven that this area can be strengthened through regular use, just as it can be weakened by being left unused. The more disciplined choices you make, the stronger your prefrontal cortex becomes. A good way to start taking advantage of this information is to start building in small willpower based decisions in your daily life. Start having a regular wake up time that you will stick to. Decide the day before what treats you are allowed and stick to it – this is a great way to avoid impulsiveness. It's easy to think or feel like you need a day off from the gym when you're trying to psyche yourself up to go. It's easy to claim you deserve a cheat meal at the end of a hard day too. Make these decisions the day before and you'll be making them clearheaded. Do you really need a break? Do you deserve a treat? If so, great! If not, plan not to do it and stick to that decision. You can quickly build some strong willpower in a short time by doing this, but you must stick to it every day otherwise it won't work.

Like I said before, if you take some time off or are on holiday mode, you should keep a couple of good willpower forming habits active so you're still ready to perform when you return to work mode. Similarly, if you're starting from a base of low willpower and want to strengthen your willpower muscle, you can start with simple habits that will help it to grow. Some ideas you can use for starters might be to avoid junk food entirely, pushing yourself through intense exercise sessions, or to force yourself to have a cold shower every day. Each and every day you should be making yourself do something for the greater good of your life, something that goes against your current impulses for comfort and security. This will force you to grow a little every day, and within weeks your willpower could be huge compared to what it is now.

MEASURING WILLPOWER

Let me start off by telling you now – there's no real way to measure exactly how much willpower a person has. What we do know though is that everybody has a set amount. This can be made bigger or smaller depending on how much you practice working on it, because the prefrontal cortex can be strengthened/weakened, but there is only a finite amount of willpower within each person. Think of it as a willpower tank – everybody has a different sized tank. You can make yours a little bigger or smaller each day by doing the right things, and each day (should) start with a full tank. This can be affected by general stress, lack of willpower over a prolonged time, substance abuse, and even lack of sleep and poor nutrition.

Always remember that your body and mind are part of the wonderful machine that is you. Like all machines though, you need to be maintained and looked after. To keep your machine in the best possible shape, you have to cover all areas from nutrition to exercise to sleep. With a well maintained machine, all of your various fuel tanks and meters should be maxed out, including your willpower tank. Ideally it will be full each morning and ready for another day.

I knew an amazing athlete once who performed at an international level. This guy did a great job of maintaining himself and staying at optimum performance levels. The reason

I was working with him though was because there was some inconsistency in his discipline over the last 12 months. Tournament performances were sometimes worse than expected and diet could be hit and miss, a confusing phenomenon with a usually well-disciplined top athlete. When we first began working together, I looked through his schedules and diaries to see if there was any info I could use to explain what was going on. Everything looked quite normal, all the planners had his training intensity peaking at the right times, recovery looked good, all should have been fine.

With no answer coming from the diaries, we needed to try a different approach. What I did was I travelled with this athlete to his next tournament and spent some time staying with him. Not all the time, because I wouldn't want to distract his focus, but enough to see that the unfamiliar bed setup caused sleep problems, which meant our athlete wasn't recovering in the best way possible.

When we began talking about his sleep setup, I discovered that he'd also been through a number of stressful events recently, including a house move. All of this had eroded his general willpower and on further examination of his diary and interviews, we found that the occasional slips in diet or training could all be linked to stressful events or times when the athlete was generally worn down. In all these cases, his willpower tank wasn't being fully refreshed each day, and he was being handicapped. His prefrontal cortex was worn down and couldn't stick to the decisions it wanted to.

This shows you the importance of managing your mind, body, and lifestyle to create an efficient machine. If an elite athlete can be derailed by minor effects capping their willpower, then anyone can. It's best to be as well rested and healthy as possible, taking an overall approach to success and self-development. Now, let's get back to that willpower meter.

Studies have shown that as we go through the day, a person becomes more likely to make bad and impulsive decisions. They're most likely to make impulse decisions late in the day, because willpower is exhausted. I believe this links back to why many successful people are in the habit of getting up early every morning. Think about it - they make an early start and get to work with their willpower meters high. Early in the day is when they'll be most productive and getting the important work done. As the day goes on, tasks become simpler and don't require as much willpower. This type of "day design" is helpful to becoming disciplined and successful in any area. In fact, a lot of successful people advocate the approach of doing the toughest tasks first. These are people who are **known** for strong willpower and achieving success, people like the Richard Bransons and Warren Buffets of this world. Surely they know what they're talking about, right?

Now that you know your willpower is finite, you know that you need to manage it in the best way possible. Laying out your day with the toughest tasks first is a great start. It also takes advantage of momentum, which plays a big part as well. See, if you start off the day with bad decisions, then it's harder to get back on track because you've already gone against your prefrontal cortex. If you overrule it on minor decisions like getting out of bed (by having a lie-in) or not eating breakfast, you create negative momentum.

This means you're more likely to make bad decisions – your willpower has almost been deactivated because you bypassed it. Imagine the person who starts off the day by snoozing the alarm multiple times, putting off when they have to get up. This person is also staying in their pyjamas instead of getting dressed. Imagine they have a mostly free day but with a little work to do, or cleaning, or even chores. How likely are they to eventually get these tasks done? Let's say they actually pull it off, are they likely to go the extra mile, get more stuff done, or put some time into self-improvement? No, because negative momentum is going to limit them to the bare minimum.

On the flipside, if you start the day with some minor momentum builders (like making your bed, taking a shower, taking out the trash), then you can put yourself in a stronger position to complete tough tasks. Positive momentum creates more belief, a stronger will, and a higher level of discipline. This is helpful if you want to have a productive day, allowing you to ease yourself into the first big tasks while still getting them done before your willpower gauge empties out. To go against our earlier example, imagine a person who always bounces out of bed at the first alarm, gets washed and ready, dresses nice, even smells good. Now imagine this person has a free(ish) day with some chores to do as well (or work, cleaning, etc.). It's easy to imagine this person just getting on with it and getting the job done, right? Try to imagine the opposite. This energetic being who bounces up and gets the early tasks done no matter what – how likely do you think they are to go and sit down, ignoring what they should be doing, and just spend the rest of the day watching TV? Come on, if you got up, got dressed, cleaned your room, and made your bed all within an hour of waking up, then you're probably going to ride that momentum a little longer and get everything done, leaving a guilt-free evening for you to enjoy.

HABITS AND ROUTINES

There are ways to boost your total amount of willpower by strengthening the rational decision-making area of your brain. We will look at these in more detail during Part Two. One technique that we'll look at now briefly is meditation. Regular meditation has been shown to reshape the prefrontal cortex, increasing its efficiency and how strongly the area can affect your brain.

Reducing cortisol (the stress hormone) also lowers your stress levels and lets you be more efficient and durable. Higher stress levels drain your energy and willpower tanks, so the practice of meditation gives benefits in two areas. It lowers your cortisol and strengthens the prefrontal cortex.

If you want to learn more about meditation, check out my other books. We've already created a few to help you with mindfulness and meditation, both of which have been directly linked to improving willpower. Not only that, willpower can also be recharged and replenished with these techniques (and others), but again, we'll get to those in the second part.

For now we are going to focus on how you can make your willpower last longer. The simplest answer is to use it more sparingly. Now that probably doesn't make sense to a lot of you – we've just been talking about using willpower to build the muscle and not letting it waste   yet now I'm telling you not to use it??

No, that's not what I'm saying at all. What I'm saying is that you can get through your life with the same good decisions (which require willpower to make), and you can do it in a way that uses less and less willpower over time. What am I talking about? I'm talking about leveraging the power of habits and making the most out of using routines.

A habit is something that you do almost automatically. It can be almost any type of action, but by becoming a habit, the conscious thought and decision-making process is normally inactive when you perform the task. Decision making isn't needed so much because you've repeated the same action over and over again until it becomes ingrained. You can speed this act up by using special techniques such as a cue when the habit starts, and a reward at the end of it. Training a habit doesn't take all that long. Once the habit is successfully set, you're no longer using much willpower to perform the action.

In fact, over time it will feel strange *not* to do the habit and will cost more willpower to resist the habit than to do it. Once you've got a good habit ingrained, it now runs on autopilot and frees up your willpower (your decision-making fuel) for other uses. One of the techniques that a lot of successful people use is to build habits slowly. One small new habit each month means you add **twelve** habits by the end of the year. At the end of the year, all 12 habits are automatic and you are using willpower to make decisions outside of those habits. You can totally rewire the way you think and act by using this technique.

One thing to keep in mind here is that the willpower gauge works a bit differently to a normal fuel gauge. We already know that it's a bit like a muscle because if you don't use it, you lose it – meaning it slowly empties out over time. Good habits run mainly on auto-pilot but they do seem to maintain your high willpower level, perhaps by activating just the tiniest amount. On the flipside, if you go and make a bad choice consciously, then your willpower seems to go down. It goes back to what we said earlier about momentum. Momentum is really important to your prefrontal cortex (the willpower muscle). Willpower loves to work with momentum, so if you make a bad choice your willpower immediately wants to start goofing around and staying inactive. This means when your willpower is strong, you have to show restraint in all areas. Imagine that you're putting out some good work, being real productive. Then you decide to slack off with the diet at lunch and have some junk food. The afternoon could easily turn into a time where you ease off and get less done because you've initiated that downwards slide by messing up your diet.

Chapter 6: Mastermind Planning

Now you've got a good understanding of willpower, right? On top of that, you know how to manage it a little better with the use of habits and routines. Now it's time to take this concept to the next level. We've already talked about building up habits to create the "you" that you dream of being. One of the things we touched on was building one habit at a time, perhaps giving each 30 days so you can gradually adapt to a new way of living. This is great for a specific type of habit but there are those that should perhaps be expanded over a bigger timeline, or even shrunk down. It all depends on how tough the habit is going to be.

Habits – Small, Big and In Between

Back when I first enrolled in university I remember it being a real big system shock to suddenly be unsupervised most of the time. It wasn't like school where teachers would try to make sure you were in the right place and that you always had all of your work completed. At uni you're responsible for yourself – if you can't be bothered to work, nobody's going to make you. They'll take your fee money and let you fail your course no problem. If you care about getting ahead and want to succeed, you're going to have to get yourself in gear and start moving.

Like so many freshmen, I struggled horribly at the start of first year. It was so easy to go and party just for one more night, or take a night off and watch some movies or go see some friends. Oh and the weekend? That's family time, I needed to go home and see my parents! Living like this I quickly fell behind my classmates and started to struggle. So I built up some new habits, a healthier life and started moving forwards. For me though there were a lot of areas I wanted to change. I needed to live more hygienically and healthily. I needed to actually start working, waking up at better times, eating better, and more. Of course I picked a habit and tried to implement one each fortnight, but the list of stuff I needed to change was SO LONG!!

Then I looked at the list and it felt like I could divide it into different sections. A lot of habits came under the same kind of category, where I wanted to implement one every couple of weeks. There were a couple that seemed really tough though. I mean, eat healthily? What, all the time!? That's so hard!

This (and a couple of other things) came in the "long" category for me, because they seemed a lot harder than my usual habits. "Being fit" was another one in this section because I hadn't exercised for at least a couple of years, and I knew it was a bad idea to go from 0 to 100 physically.

Likewise, there were a couple of things that seemed a bit too easy, like brushing my teeth each morning (yes, sometimes I was THAT lazy...) or making sure to eat three meals a day. These were the "short" list, things that should be easy to change in my life.

Now while I stuck with the "one-per-fortnight" rule for most of my habit changes, for the "short" list (the easy list), I tried to change one habit **every three days**. You can use a different timescale if you want, but it's not too tough to make a little change every few days. Layer them up and they'll stay with you because they're easier things to do, so they use less willpower. These small habits build up side-by-side while your main habit also changes.

Then we have the difficult list, the "long" changes. For these you should break it down into steps and move through one step every few weeks. Don't add a new step in this habit at the same time as you add a new main habit. So if you are adding a new habit at the start of each month, add a new "step" for the long/hard habit at mid-month. It keeps you from feeling overwhelmed.

I did this to add 30 mins of exercise every couple weeks. At first I was only working out for half hour – easy, right? But two months later I was hitting the gym four times a week for half hour and feeling pretty great. Four months in my habit was built and I had three to four weekly sessions of almost an hour. By the end of first year I was much fitter than at the start, and entering my second year, I was in the best shape of my life.

BUILDING YOUR FUTURE SELF

When it comes to achieving your dreams in life, it's all a matter of planning and action. Everything else comes as a by-product of those two things. Peyton Manning, one of the greatest quarterbacks in the history of American Football, once said:

"I never left the field saying I could have done more to get ready and that gives me peace of mind."

This guy was an 18-year veteran of the NFL and at the top of the game from beginning to end. He never stopped working and was a strong impact player even in his final years. His work ethic is what made him so good, but look at this part of the quote – "done more to get ready." It's talking about his prep work. He wasn't just a hard worker, he was a smart one too. He studied the opposition defences, learned their tendencies, and memorized any weak points. It was a smart approach, and he combined it with hard work to ingrain the tendencies of every opposition defence into his mind. This is how he maximized his potential through hard, smart work. The level of intensity he used with this approach is unreal. He was once quizzed by a journalist on a playbook he used 16 years earlier in his career. He still remembered every detail, right down to the personnel and timings. His depth of preparation keeps the details in his mind decades after they're needed!

To achieve your dreams, you need to do the same kind of thing. Everybody has the potential within them. MMA great Conor McGregor famously said:

"I'm not talented, I'm obsessed."

This quote shows how much weight he puts into his self-belief and discipline, into his work rate and intense preparation. It shows his belief that innate talent doesn't really matter and that **anyone** can build themselves to be whatever they want.

When you understand that, you need to have a long and hard think about what it is you want out of life. These goals are achievable, but it takes the right approach, the right kind of lifestyle. To put it simply, if you want to be a millionaire you have to behave like a millionaire. I don't mean spending lots of money and dressing well. I mean putting in the millionaire hours – those early mornings and late nights, those meetings outside of work to build your own business or deals. Figure out what habits will take you where you need to go in life and create a list of what this person does, how they live and spend their time.

Now look at the difference between your own lifestyle and this "target lifestyle." What needs to be changed? Make a list so you can refer back to it. At the start, it can be very general and sprawling, but you slowly want to structure it into those changes that need to be made – the "big," "small," and "medium." Now you can work on making these changes and building new habits one at a time. Like a sculptor you begin to shape your future self, creating these new habits and getting closer to the life you dream of. Along the way, again like a sculptor, there's another point to keep in mind.

"Hack away at the unessential." – Bruce Lee

Bruce Lee is a legend all over the world. A martial arts superstar, actor, and philosopher, Bruce had an immense impact on the world despite his untimely demise at the young age of 32. The above quote sums up one of his core beliefs – that many people are worried about what they can add, when they could easily benefit from removing things instead. His meaning? Bad habits!

Bad habits are a drain on you because they cause setbacks and have no real positive payoff. Sure it might feel good to eat some more junk food or sleep in on weekends, but outside of the short term pleasure, is it actually getting you any closer to your goals? Or is it keeping them a little further away?

You have to consider your bad habits and decide whether they make sense to keep or not. Then approach them in the same way as the good habits – try to get rid of one at a time. Doing this helps to speed the process of creating your future self along. It's a double pronged approach where you combine building good habits with removing the bad ones. Changes will happen a lot faster than if you just took one approach or the other.

SCHEDULES

Another way you can get the most out of your willpower is by using schedules. This is different from a habit. A habit has to be constant, something that takes place regularly. This is like a wake-up time or sticking to an exercise plan. It works for regular events, but not everything in life is regular.

Most people have to put in some extra work to succeed in life. This is how they launch businesses and brands or create a product to sell. It's pretty tough to do any of that when you're on the clock at work, because you have other tasks to be busy with. Even if you can get away with it, it might be a bad idea to try. Most employers will be pretty displeased if they find out, and it could even cost you your job.

The reason most people struggle to put in effort outside of work is because they lack mental discipline. They will never admit this though, always blaming a lack of time instead. The truth is that we all have the same amount of time in a day. If you want to have a life that most people can't, then you have to do what most people are unwilling to do – put the extra time in.

I totally understand that a job can be tiring. Days can be long and hard. At the end you'll probably be tired and the idea of more work can be depressing. With your own ideas the work isn't straight forward either. You need to decide what to do first and the best way to approach it. Then there's other life issues to deal with – doing chores, socializing, exercising. Having all of this to deal with when you're already tired from work would be intimidating for anyone. Your willpower tank is low and the idea of sorting through this mess will make the brain want to start cutting things out, avoiding the difficulty and discomfort of getting things done.

You can help your brain here though, and you can stretch that willpower a little bit further. What you need to do is use a schedule.

A schedule is like prep work for your day. You can do it first thing in the morning, but it's usually best to make it the night before. Regular events like work and a morning routine are quite easy to work in. After those are filled in, you can add any appointments, meetings, or social events too. This gives a good overview of your day so you can see what down time should be available.

Always remember to give yourself adequate time for everything otherwise a schedule can backfire and cause you more stress as you fall behind on it. Things like travel times, traffic, and other delays need to be taken into account as well.

Now what you need to do is fill in the blank parts with activities that are going to push you towards your goals. That doesn't mean you have to be constantly working either though – feel free to have some scheduled downtime when needed. Practising good self-care is a vital part of discipline. Just like a machine, you need to be operating at your best for everything to work properly. Neglect your maintenance and it's a matter of time before a breakdown occurs.

By filling in those blank spaces with something productive, you make sure that you're moving in the right direction. You've already made the decision of what to do (and when) beforehand, so your willpower muscle isn't needed as much to get you started. Even when you're tired, it's easy to look at a schedule and get on with the next job on your list. This saves a little bit of willpower, but more importantly it gets rid of the daunting feeling that people get when they're unsure of how they're going to fit everything in.

CHUNKING

Your schedule gives you the task to concentrate on, so don't worry about what comes after. Just do what's in front of you. This is **chunking** in a different way, and it keeps your brain relaxed. Staying relaxed and keeping cortisol low lets you exercise more willpower too. It's all about harnessing the power of your mind, instead of letting your mind rule you.

If you have a big, complex task to do then break it down into smaller steps. These smaller steps can be broken down even more if you need to. Just get it to a point where every step you need to take can be translated into a task for your schedule. This is also chunking. In fact, we're going to look at chunking in a few different ways.

By breaking down your bigger plan into small steps, you create manageable chunks. It's a lot of work to write an epic novel for example, but it's not too difficult to write a couple of pages. Repeat that action enough times though and you have a book. Couple it with some planning stages and some editing and you have a decent book. From there it's a matter of learning, working on your craft, and adjusting. Ultimately though, you've achieved a tough goal by breaking it down into tiny chunks.

Doing this is another way to get rid of that scary feeling that big jobs cause. Now you know how to use chunking for big jobs and to get through your schedule. Sometimes you might be struggling outside of those specific areas too. People can get tired, or sick, or be in extremely stressful circumstances. Maybe the job at hand is just one, long slog that can't really be broken down because it's similar work over a long period.

This is where you can use chunking as a mental trick. Keep in mind this takes practice and self-belief. If you want to pull it off when it's needed, then you have to practice and try it as much as possible beforehand. I use this in my own fitness training. Special forces operators have brought it up as one of their tricks for getting through the gruelling selection process too. It's the ability to accept that you're going to be a little uncomfortable and just go through it for a short period of time. Start with a minute if you need to. Then do a second one.

It isn't about just taking it one minute at a time though, it's about focusing only on the minute you're in and trying to reach the end. When I practice this, it's at the end of a tough run. On a normal run, I have a target distance in mind and always hit it. Sometimes I'm tired and this is difficult to do. Say I've picked a 10km run and I'm gassed out at 6km. All I do is try to reach 7km. Then I can stop. That's literally what I tell myself, that I can stop at 7km.

When I reach it though, I know I can do a little more, so I try to hit 8km and call it quits there. I push hard, really struggling towards the end, but hitting the mark gives me another little boost. Now another 1km seems horrible. But 500m? Let's do that. Then the next 300m. Then 200 more to hit 9km. Now how can I not try for a little more, being so close to the end?

In the case of a special forces soldier, sometimes the end isn't even known. Sometimes they're being pursued or have already been captured. In these situations if you can't stay positive, you might end up dead – and it's a tough situation to stay positive in. Again though, these people break down time into whatever chunks necessary. It could be the next day, hour, or even the next five seconds. What matters is to stay calm and focused on the goal, positive that something will succeed if you stay the course. By doing this, they survive day-long firefights and months after being captured. People have traversed entire deserts over weeks on foot by taking everything one step at a time. There's no reason you can't break that tough task down, taking it one moment at a time, and do the same.

CHAPTER 7: INTELLIGENCE VERSUS EMOTION

With the creation of your masterplan, you have a goal. By breaking it down into steps and taking smart action, you can begin the journey towards your goal. We've talked in the last chapter about growing as a person and taking steps along your journey, building good habits and getting rid of bad ones. To make sure this is all working properly though, you need to be aware of how you're progressing.

SELF-ANALYSIS

For most people, it's easy to underestimate or overestimate how well they're doing. This is an area where your intelligence has to be used, rather than your emotion. Emotions are feelings. I'm the kind of guy who is very demanding on myself. My emotions usually make me feel as though I'm not doing enough. Unfortunately, that means I can overload myself with work and really struggle to get through my schedule sometimes. This has a bad effect on my mentality, because I start to feel overwhelmed and downhearted about falling behind. In truth, my work rate is usually above where it needs to be – it's just the way I'm wired means I always feel like I need to do more.

On the other hand, some people (maybe most) are wired to believe they're doing more than they actually are. For these people, even taking a couple of steps makes it feel like they're progressing towards their goal. Even one step is better than nothing so they're right of course – they are progressing. Question is, are they moving at the speed they want to? Probably not.

You should always be taking an objective look at how you're performing in all areas of life. Are you making good schedules that aren't too easy or too demanding? Are you sticking to them? Have you been forming good habits and sticking to them, just how your plan says you should? Have you been dropping the bad ones? Or have you been a little lazy at times, perhaps with a couple of slip ups?

Remember everybody makes mistakes. Changing your mind and your life isn't as simple as flicking a switch. It takes time and consistent effort. If you mess up a couple of times or let your standards slide a little, that's okay. The important thing is to be moving forward and at a decent speed. Analyze your performance and habits, take stock of what you're sticking to and what you're failing at. Be honest about it, because you are doing this **for you!**

If you need to sharpen up a couple of habits or change your approach, do it! It takes an honest, analytical approach to make the most of your new mentality. Everybody slacks off sometimes and everybody makes mistakes. That's how life is, and it's how we learn and grow. What matters is that you sit down, look over your schedules, notes, and other plans, and then be honest about your progress. Being honest with yourself is massively important if you want to succeed!

Using analysis like this can give you a boost too. It'll show you what you're doing well and which points you're sticking to. Knowing this and comparing it to your schedules from a few months back can show an incredible amount of growth in that time. You really can make huge changes without much effort if you break those changes down into steps and use a smart plan.

How Emotions Affect Performance

Listen to anybody who has to perform professionally in a stressful environment and they'll tell you that emotional control is vital. For athletes, soldiers, and business owners all over the world, emotion can have a massive effect. These are the professions where we can see the effects most easily. A sportsman putting in a bad performance is more likely to lose their temper than one performing well. This is down to the frustration they feel with being shut down or unable to perform.

Back in the 80's and 90's, Mike Tyson was absolutely demolishing the professional boxing scene. Between 1985 and 1996, Tyson went on a tear, losing only once. Outside of an upset loss to Buster Douglas, "Iron Mike" had won every fight to achieve a 45-1 record. Of those 45 wins, only 5 men had survived to see the final bell. Then came the fights against Evander Holyfield...

In the first fight, Holyfield shut Tyson down in the clinch. He bent the rules and used some controversial tactics to stifle Tyson and take the win. In the rematch, he opened up in the same way. Tyson quickly became frustrated and responded by biting off a piece of Holyfield's ear. This got him disqualified and banned from boxing.

Years later, Oprah would interview Tyson and ask what happened. Here is Mike's answer:

"I was angry that he was butting me. He cut my head in the first fight and then did it again. I was angry and in a rage. It's no excuse for what happened, but I wanted to inflict pain on him. I was just p*ss*d off that he was such a great fighter too, wanted to just beat him up."

Boxing is a combat sport. Both men are trying to hurt each other and land punches. Here you can see one of the all-time greats talk about how angry and riled up he was because he was facing a better opponent. He lost his composure and his temper, leading to a disgraceful incident and a big career loss.

Situations like this happen all over the world in sports. Novak Djokovic destroying rackets, Zinedane Zidane landing a headbutt, and the Pacers and Pistons brawling on court – all of these are examples of emotion getting the better of people.

In every one of those situations, we're talking about top level athletes. These people know the intelligent approach to competing in their sports. They have discipline and drive, and they are able to break things down and deal with the problem at hand. They know how to be mentally tough and how to use their willpower, since these are both key traits for elite athletes. The problem in these situations is their emotional control.

Emotions can have their place when it comes to performance. Earlier on I mentioned Mike Tyson's only loss in those first 11 years of his career. It came against Buster Douglas in 1990, at a time when Tyson was considered unstoppable and the Douglas was considered more of a gatekeeper than championship material. The fight was supposed to be a tune up for Tyson, an easy win before he moved on to a big money bout.

For Douglas though, this was the biggest fight of his career. He was training hard for it every day, putting everything he could into it with the aim of making his mother proud. A few weeks before the fight, Douglas' mother unfortunately passed away, leaving him in a highly emotional state.

When an athlete has a meltdown and loses their cool, it's due to emotion – often because of a bad performance, or mind games from the opposition/fans. Other times it's down to frustration at not being good enough or bad refereeing. All of these situations can cause a bad emotional reaction and have negative effects.

On the flipside, there are many athletes who achieve success **because of emotion**. There are plenty of people who came from bad circumstances to achieve success. Ray Lewis, Floyd Mayweather Jr., and Lebron James are all examples of rags to riches stories. For these people, the bad childhoods and negative emotions became fuel. It gave them the intensity to reach the top and stay there, to be the best in their field. Harnessing emotion in this way brought them success.

Buster Douglas did the same thing when his mother died. He harnessed it into his last couple of weeks in training camp. Then he kept it in mind during the fight too, unafraid of Tyson's attacks and fighting his own fight. In most of Tyson's earlier fights, his opponents were intimidated by his reputation, his physique, and his aggression. Mentally they were already weak before the opening bell had been rung. Douglas wasn't like them though, or at least he wasn't after the untimely death of his mother. She was a proud woman and had been bragging to all of her friends that Buster was going to beat Mike Tyson. Now with her gone, all he wanted was to give her this last parting gift – the gift of making her right and doing what she had hoped for.

Combine this with how emotion was messing with Tyson. He was overly confident and relaxed, convinced that this would be another easy win. Having seen so much success in the last few years, Tyson had taken it easy in training and was fighting with almost no strategy. He loaded up over and over again, looking for that one big shot to end the night. Douglas stayed disciplined, held his distance, and dug deep a couple of times when he looked to be in trouble. He was even knocked down in the 9th round but managed to barely beat the count and keep himself in the fight. From there, he made history in the 10th round by knocking Mike Tyson down – and becoming the first man to beat him. Tyson failed to beat the count and lost by KO, a single blemish with five years of perfect success either side of it. When asked how he was able to win, Buster answered:

"Because of my mother."

It's a perfect example of how emotion can be harnessed and made to have a positive effect on performance.

Now you can see that emotions can have good effects, or bad effects. It doesn't even matter what emotion is being felt at the time because anger has been channelled positively and negatively by people everywhere. The same is true of difficulties in life and frustration. It's true for sadness, grief, and despair. Any emotion can impact how we think and behave.

Two different people can come from very similar backgrounds and end up entirely different based on *how they react* to situations. One person may take bad events and be negative, becoming a hopeless person who falls into a destructive cycle. The other might use the negativity *as fuel* to propel them forwards – determined not to be put in such a bad situation again. It all comes down to what *you* decide to make of your life.

THE EVOLUTION OF THE HUMAN BRAIN

Most animals in existence have a brain. There are some that don't have a brain, because they don't need one. A sea sponge is an example of a living creature without a brain. These sponges have stayed on the ocean floor for millions of years, filtering out particles of food and nutrition from the water around them. The filtering happens automatically – they never have any decision to make, there's no need to be aware of their surroundings, and they don't need any sensory organs or the ability to move.

This is why they work so well without a brain – it doesn't help them to function or live any better than they can already. For this type of creature, a brain would just be an extra drain on its resources, because for most creatures, it's the brain that takes the most energy to power. Sea sponges were the earliest branch to split off from other animals in general, and they have had very little reason to evolve since then, benefitting from simplicity and effectiveness.

How is all of this relevant to you? Somewhere along the line, billions of years ago, all (or most) living things had a common ancestor. Go back far enough and you'll find a simple organism, one that was probably capable of finding energy/food sources and reproducing. It would have lacked a brain initially and been able to perform only simple tasks to survive and reproduce.

As time went by, this organism would have mutated and evolved. It would have split into a few different lines, each one evolving differently. One of these ancient lines was that of the sea sponges. They can survive for a long time and have had no need to evolve, living a simple and boring existence. Other lines became more complicated and adaptable.

A lot of the evolutions from this organism would have been into bigger, more complicated organisms – the creatures that inhabit todays earth and oceans. These creatures would have been the ones that developed a brain, sensory organs, and mobile lifestyles. Most of our origins can be traced back to the ocean, where life began on this planet. Different types of creatures would have roamed the ocean back then with all kinds of weird and wonderful designs.

For mobile creatures, let's use the average, ancient fish as an example. This animal would need to swim through the water, navigating it accurately. It would need to be able to hunt or otherwise find food in this environment and has to actually eat something rather than draw nutrient particles from the water. Again, this bigger need for energy is because there's so much more to power – the sensory organs, the digestive system, the decision-making brain, the muscles of the body for movement, the circulatory system to keep everything operational – the list goes on and on!

While the brain has so much more to do in this creature, a lot of it must still happen automatically. This is because the **animal brain does not have the awareness of a human brain**. In most animals, the brain is wired to make specific decisions based on the situation around them.

A great example of this can be seen in ladybugs, or ladybird beetles. These insects are quite harmless and easy to catch if you come across one. They have wings but don't use them unless there's a reason. Most of the time, the ladybug will calmly walk around and explore if no danger or food are detected in the area. If you place a leaf, your hand, or any other item directly into the path of the bug it will continue walking straight on to whatever you placed there. This is because they only process whether they can continue in a straight line or not. They don't have the ability to pre-plan a route, or to remember where they've been. It's like a computer program – it asks, "Is there a path directly ahead?" If there is, it follows it.

Get one of these bugs on a stick and it will walk to the end, see the path has ended, and turn around. It will then repeat the process. When it first turns, you must have your hand or something else at the end of the stick, so the bug sees a path off the stick. It will begin the route and not process any further information – like that the path has disappeared. It only notices this when it hits the end. At that time, it looks for another path and heads towards it. You can keep a bug walking on the same stick for a long time in this way because it won't remember anything. Instead of using memory, it works purely from what it can see/smell/sense, as it was hard-wired to do.

On the other hand, a human brain can remember. It can also visualize things and see potential dangers around you – you don't need to touch the fire to know it's dangerous. The animal brain is hard-wired for survival but can be beaten because it only has one criteria of responses. The human brain doesn't; it is much more intelligent and has many ways to respond to a situation.

So the human brain is better, right? Well, in some ways. Before we had our complex human brains, we had simpler animal brains, which were hard-wired for survival. The animal brain cares only about survival and will react in very predictable ways. The human brain is more about adaptation, understanding, and making the most out of a situation. Somewhere along our evolutionary history, we began to switch from one to the other...

THE ANIMAL BRAIN VERSUS THE HUMAN BRAIN

Modern day humans can suffer a lot from the evolutionary hangover of an animal brain. With the human brain, it seems we didn't just switch from one type to the other. The human brain is the most incredible and complex organ in existence. We still don't truly understand how the entire brain works, which is why brain surgery is so delicate and why brain injuries can be so devastating and hard to treat. It's literally easier to code a supercomputer than it is to decode the brain.

What we know is that the brain has evolved gradually over millions of years and that it differs from the brains of other animals. At the core of our brains is the **basal ganglia region**, an area which has been likened to the reptile brain by some neuroscientists. This area of the brain is the deepest, so logically it should be the oldest. If we look at birds and reptiles, whose brains have similar structures to this area, we see animals that function mostly on instinct. These animals will seek food, shelter, and heat sources. They have a very basic social structure and not much in the way of family ties. They are wired to survive, feed, and reproduce. A creature of this type only makes very basic decisions, such as whether to challenge a rival for a mate or not based on the likelihood of winning. There's no real memory or advanced decision making involved.

Outside of the basal ganglia are more advanced systems like the amygdalae and the hypothalamus. Research has shown that these are the areas of the brain that allow us to create memories. They're also responsible for our emotions and our hormone systems. These regions of the brain can be described as parts of the **limbic system**, a term that was originally used by neuroscientist Paul MacLean. He proposed that this part of the brain developed as our ancestors diverged away from the reptilian ways of life and became more like modern mammals.

These animals would have had the ability to feel basic emotions and to remember past events. This basic level of memory would then allow them to avoid dangers and remember family members. Along with the existence of emotions and a hormonal system, these animals could feel preferences for different foods, individuals, or areas to shelter in. Hard-wired responses are no longer the normal way of life for this animal. It can still make decisions based on survival instincts and these are affected by the existence of memories. This animal can also make emotional decisions though, because the system has now become advanced – an example would be the existence of family groups.

Often a family group will stay together and look after each other, the stronger members taking care of the weaker ones. Parenting first becomes a real feature around these times with older animals guarding and nurturing their offspring. In the past, a strong individual would go solo to maximize their own chance of survival, but now they would remain part of the group to maximize the chance of the family genetics surviving. The shift from hard-wired response to actually processing information and making a decision is well underway.

Finally, the most advanced brain region was created – **the neocortex**. This part of the brain is only found in higher mammals and is the area that allows us humans to have language, the ability to perceive information and learn from the information of others. It gives us the ability to create plans and designs, to draw conclusions from raw information provided to us, and to have a constant awareness of the world around us at all times.

The developments to this stage of the human brain allow us to be the intelligent super-beings we are – but the other parts of the brain still exist. These more primitive areas are still involved in how we live day to day, and they still affect us greatly – after all, they've been there for millennia and have successfully kept our genetic line alive until today.

These parts of the brain are still very basic and they act accordingly. They are still hard-wired to avoid danger, pain, and discomfort. The problem is that to get ahead in modern life, **you sometimes have to face discomfort, risk, or pain**. If there wasn't any risk or pain involved in achieving success, everybody would do it, right?

UNDERSTANDING THE INSTINCTUAL BRAIN

Evolution has wired your brain to avoid negative emotions and experiences. It does this because it wants to keep you (the host animal) happy, healthy, and alive. The happier you are, the better your life will be.

Unfortunately, the animal brain doesn't understand the concept of planning for the future. It only understands the here and now.

At the highest levels of your human brain, you can understand that sacrificing some pleasure now can pay off in the long-term. Going through some discomfort today in the form of work, effort, and discipline can bring you a bigger payoff in the future. Your human brain knows this and can create a plan for you to follow. Follow the plan and you can have the future you dream of.

The animal brain doesn't understand this plan. It only understands what's in front of it right now – in this case that would be work. It recognizes work as an unpleasant activity with no immediate pay-off because it doesn't give you any food, shelter, or anything to reproduce with. To the animal brain, work is a fruitless exercise that only brings discomfort and wastes your energy. Much better to stay resting and enjoying yourself until you need to do something more useful.

One of the biggest parts of mental discipline is overcoming and outsmarting the animal brain. You have to take control on a conscious level and start living your life to the plan of your human brain instead of living instinctually.

When you feel resistance to putting in extra work, it's your animal brain trying to protect you and keep you happy. When you feel nervous about trying a new venture or hesitant about taking a calculated risk that's needed for your plan, it's because your animal brain is trying to avoid danger and uncertainty. It's so worried about failure that it will try to keep you from trying in the first place. You'll feel mental blocks and uncertainty. You will feel stressed as well sometimes, and that's normal when you're trying to resist millennia of hard-wired instinct.

By understanding why these feelings come up, you can begin to overcome them. Procrastination is a big one, with so many people putting off any work until the last possible minute. Why? So if it isn't of the highest quality, they already have an excuse. In this case, the animal brain isn't even protecting you physically anymore, it's protecting you mentally and emotionally. The instinctive brain will avoid any and all negatives, whether they are real physical dangers or imagined mental ones. It will avoid any situations where you could face embarrassment or difficulty. It will do everything possible to keep you in a safe and secure situation, one where you aren't challenged or threatened in any way.

The problem with this is that growth comes outside of your comfort zones, and success requires an extraordinary effort, which automatically means you have to exit the comfort zone!

To overcome your instinctual habits, you should be very conscious of what you are doing and why. Don't resist what your instincts want to do; instead accept the feeling but with an understanding of why it exists. Allow it to be there and take a mindful approach to focus on the minor pain of what you *need* to do and the major payoff when it works. Your instincts will become more aligned with your mind by doing this, allowing you to live more productively.

The use of calming techniques and mindfulness will lessen the intensity of the negative feelings your instincts create. Relaxing yourself and understanding these feelings reduces their impact and allows you to stay more in the moment. By being in the moment, you can truly understand and accept that nothing all that bad is going to happen to you. Doing a little work isn't as horrible as your instincts might believe, and by focusing on the eventual payoff and your reasons for doing this, you can create positive momentum and motivation.

Living to the plan of your higher brain is your true path to pleasure and success; it's the path your instincts should be following, but they don't know that. Times have changed rapidly and our evolutionary instincts are lagging behind. These days it's all about risk management and moving forward, taking the extra steps needed to reach your dreams.

I once asked one of my university professors how he could have continued higher education for a decade before beginning his profession. With all the studying, the exams and the dissertations, wasn't he tired and bored? Was it worth it just to have multiple PhD's? To him it was. To him, every year and every semester was another step to his masterplan. It was all leading to what he wanted – to be the most sought after specialist in his country for his particular area of knowledge. He knew that by being that, he could have the life he wanted. His work could be focused on his passion, day after day. His financial compensation would be plenty, enough for him to live his dreams and secure the wellbeing of his family. His life would have the balance he craved and he would be proud of all of his achievements.

For him, this dream was worth a decade of uncomfortable learning and working, grinding away at his craft. For him, the instinctive brain was overcome early and his higher thinking brain was able to shape the life he wanted. Today he lives happily, just as he deserves to, and continues to educate future generations on psychology and human behavior.

Now you have a better understanding of why it can be hard to stay disciplined, even though you know it's the better option for you. With an awareness of why this happens, you can begin to resist the thoughts and feelings that could cause you to slack off. Stay aware of the long-term pain and costs of being lazy and not reaching your goals. Keep a slight focus on them through your day-to-day life and you'll start to notice automatic motivation appearing within you. You'll be able to stay disciplined much more easily if you begin to associate lack of discipline with lasting, long-term pain. Always remember that short-term pleasure is meaningless if it distracts you from long-term goals.

CHAPTER 8: CONTROLLING THE MIND

Mind control is the kind of superpower everybody would like to have. Being able to control minds and the way they think is pretty much the same as controlling people's actions. A person acts on their thoughts, so before they can do something, they must think it. Of course people can act quite instinctively or subconsciously, but these decisions are created either by *habit* or by automatic reactions based on past events – so your brain already decided it knows the best response without needing you to consciously think.

There is no special device or trick that will allow you to control the minds of other people. Being able to control your own mind is a superpower in its own way. I'm sure you're already thinking that you have control over your own mind, but if you had true control, you wouldn't need the advice in this book. No, true mind control comes when you are able to dismiss any irrelevant thoughts. It comes when you have complete control over your mental focus, when you are able to dismiss intrusive or unhelpful thoughts and instantly replace them with empowering ones. Once you reach this level of control, discipline becomes easier. This is because thoughts of the short-term pain no longer enter your mind, only of the long-term pain associated with NOT being disciplined. The same thing happens with pleasure as you focus on the long-term pleasure from reaching your goals instead of the short term pleasure of slacking off.

KNOWING YOURSELF

The first step to getting control over your thoughts and your mind is to become aware of them. There is an ancient Greek saying of unknown origins that says:

"Know thyself."

This saying goes back many decades, though nobody knows exactly how old it is or who originally said it. The quote was inscribed at the Temple of Apollo in Delphi, which was believed to have been constructed by the 4th century B.C. at the latest, so this saying is at least roughly 2400 years old already. A lot of people underestimate the importance of this quote or misunderstand what it means in the first place.

"Know thyself? Of course I know myself!" – this is the way of thinking so many people have when they first come across this quote. Over the years, knowing yourself has been given more importance than knowing your enemy or rival. Sun Tzu attached great importance to knowing both yourself and your enemy. Sun Tzu was a tactical genius, an expert in the matters of combat and warfare. For him, it was vital that he knew as much as possible about his enemies – their habits and tendencies, their strengths and weaknesses, their beliefs, their loves, fears, and anything else he could learn about them. Having a complete knowledge was what could give him the edge in the battlefield.

He also knew that he needed to know himself. He understood his own tendencies and preferences and analyzed them as an observer – without any attachment or emotion. He would search for his own weaknesses and accept them. He would find his own strengths, too, and by knowing both his strengths and weaknesses, he was able to steer the battle into situations that favored him over his enemies.

Sun Tzu knew that sometimes your own weaknesses meant you should not attack your opponents' weak points. At other times, your strengths may make it possible to attack your opponent at his strongest point. It didn't come down to the simple approach of knowing what is strong versus what is weak; it came down to knowing how your own strengths/weaknesses match up against the opposition in different areas. This way you can find where you have the biggest advantage over your opponent, even it isn't your best strength. This is what knowing yourself means.

Beyond that, knowing yourself is also about honesty. If you tend to be flustered in the face of challenges, you need to know and accept this beforehand. Ignoring it can put you in a dangerous situation.

Long ago I was taken out on a team-building exercise with a group of my colleagues. In the business world, we take a lot of parallels from war and the military. The fact that Sun Tzu is considered such a huge influence in the modern business world is a great example of this. On the team-building exercise, we were practicing this in full – it was an event ran by former military personnel and based on a military theme. Our challenge at the time was to transport a bunch of equipment across some difficult terrain and in harsh conditions. As part of the brief, we were told that we had to complete the mission in a certain timeframe because we were being hunted by the enemy.

The key to accomplishing this mission was good teamwork. More than teamwork, it was important to know the team and to maximize their performance by splitting jobs up properly. When the task began, we didn't know any of this. So, what did we do?

Obviously we tried to keep things equal, because that's what modern day society has told us. We live in a time where equality and fairness are being pushed massively. Everybody is told that they have the ability and right to do anything that any other person can.

At a fundamental level, this is true of course – we all start off with similar levels of potential. I believe that *almost* any young child can be trained and taught to be a high achiever in any field if the right approach is taken. What I don't believe is that any/every adult is capable of producing what another adult is. Over our lives, we are all shaped by circumstances and take on different traits and abilities. A child is like a blank slate, and while they may have slightly different talents, most of them have massive potential. An adult has already begun to learn his limits and no longer has that useful ability to absorb information and learn rapidly.

We all have different skills and strengths, different ways of handling issues, and different weaknesses. It's what makes us all individuals, and it's actually what allows us humans to be successful as a society – because our strength doesn't come from individuals, it comes from the unity and togetherness of our society.

Modern day scientists are building on the work of the experts who came before them, allowing them to take the next step and move our society forwards. For example, we have the world's greatest engineering minds working on building the next generation of tech and we get the most out of them by providing them with every tool and resource needed. We try to build the best possible teams around them so they can work together and build on the knowledge of those who came before them. We **don't** expect them to contribute to other areas of our society though. I mean, why would we?!

Could you imagine the waste of talent if we asked the engineer to also take part in basic construction? The engineers time and effort would be wasted on a basic job that somebody else could do, while there's nobody skilled enough to replace them in their actual job. This is an example of society using its resources wisely to make the best gains. As you can see here, humans aren't the same and they aren't equal. Each one is individual and this is something to be celebrated. No human should feel they are *better* than other people based on a skill – the basic home builder is also a vital cog in our societal machine, and they deserve admiration and appreciation. People shouldn't feel bad for having their own specialist skills and talents either though. In fact, being an individual should be embraced, because it's by having different strengths that we can create strong teams, strong businesses, and strong societies.

Now, back to our team-building mission. Our problem here was that we were so heavily invested in the idea of equality. None of us wanted to tell each other that we weren't good at things, so there was a lot of "fairness for the sake of being fair" instead of focusing on how to best do the job.

We rotated our lookouts so that everybody was on lookout duty at some point. We also rotated our lead scout so no one person had to do too much running back and forth, and we divided the responsibility of carrying the equipment equally. Every five minutes we would swap the carriers around, again making it equal.

The mission wasn't a complete disaster, but it certainly could have gone smoother. When we finished, the C.O. (Commanding Officer) went over a quick debrief with us. A few of his early questions really drove home how important it is to focus on strengths and weaknesses, then gear your plan according to those.

"Why did you have these tiny women carrying the same amount of equipment as the big 6'4" tanks?! Why didn't you let the big guys carry more so you could all move faster?!"

"What was the idea behind rotating your big guys in as scouts too? They stand out a mile coming over the horizon and it's a waste of their energy to try and zip around the terrain fast and unseen!"

"Do you not realize that by changing the lookout, you've got a new lookout coming in who doesn't know if anything just changed in the surroundings? This is their first time looking at the surroundings and terrain!"

"Why was there so much discussion and so many voices every time a decision had to be made? Where was the leadership, where was the organization?"

Each and every point was a valid one, and it seemed to make so much sense now that it was pointed out. Of course we should have just given the big guys most of the equipment, because they could carry it without becoming exhausted. If they needed a break later on, we could have swapped for a short while, but for the most part, they would have been able to move the equipment and still be in good shape – compared to a couple of our smaller members who had been left exhausted by trying to carry heavy items.

On the flipside, our big guys found it exhausting if they had to lead scout, running back and forth trying to path find and trying to relay information. They really would have been better off using their strength to carry stuff while the smaller team members saved energy, because for them, covering the ground on foot was a much easier job than carrying equipment.

The same applied for our leadership – those who were best equipped to lead should have been left to it. There should have been a better chain of command in place, allowing everybody to do what they did best, and allowing the team as a whole to finish the mission faster and to stay safer along the way.

From that day, I've always known the importance of knowing your strengths and weaknesses. You have to be extremely honest with yourself and with others. Before this exercise, I would always try my best on any job. Now I don't hesitate to pass on a project that might be better suited to somebody else. This might sound picky to some, but my success has been achieved with this method. Of course I don't limit myself or stick ONLY to what I excel at – there has to be some pushing of the boundaries since that's the way we learn and grow. I focus on what I can do well and try to build my skills from there.

When it comes to making progress in your own life, figure out what your strengths and weaknesses are and work to them. One of my past problems was procrastination. It's so easy to slack off and do the minimum when you have the space to get away with it. I became aware of this weakness, this tendency to back off if there was enough time/space to get away with it. Two of my strengths that are relevant are that I can work well to a deadline and that I'm highly productive in mornings. To leverage this, I began to schedule my work in a way that it was mostly in the mornings. Instantly there was a jump in my productivity because most of my actual work was done in the mornings, while the afternoons were more for admin, chores, and menial tasks. Structuring my life in this way took advantage of my strength at performing early in the day and allowed my weakness of slacking off later to become less of a problem. If something didn't get my full attention, at least it wasn't important enough to actually affect my life.

The other thing I had to do was accept that I wasn't going to smash out assignments ahead of their deadlines. It just didn't work for me. I could put double the amount of time in and still end up with the same work, because it was the deadline itself that helped motivate and fuel me for work. My solution here was one that worked for me, but one that some people might find highly stressful.

Again, knowing yourself is important. I knew I could handle the stress and that it would actually be a benefit to me, because it would fuel my work rate. What did I do? I started scheduling work in such a way that I had to make the most of it whenever I did sit down to work. If I didn't, there wasn't enough time assigned to get the project finished by deadline day. This **forced** me to sit and be productive each and every time and to make sure I had to stick to those time slots. I filled the rest of my time with other work, chores, social time, and self-improvement. The plan was to develop and progress in all areas of life and by restricting each one to its own time slots, I made every activity more important to myself. I knew that no matter where I was in my day, there was something else coming up on the schedule – even my relaxation time had a slot at the end of each day!

For some people, sticking to the schedule would be a problem because mine doesn't have much flexibility. Again, it comes back to knowing yourself and how you work. For me, this schedule is perfect. I like being able to look at it and have it tell me what to do or where to go. I like not having too much lax time, but I also don't schedule end-to-end so there is a little breathing space if needed.

Somebody else might like more of a vague and flexible schedule, while another person might prefer a to-do list that can be checked off in any order, rather than a strict, ordered schedule. It all comes down to knowing yourself. What will work for you? Embrace that! What won't work for you? Ditch it!

MENTAL AWARENESS

At the start of this chapter we talked about mind control and how you can create control over your own mind to enforce discipline and shape your life. The way you do this is by being aware of your thoughts and gaining control over those.

Everything starts with our thoughts. These thoughts are massively powerful because they create our words, our actions, and our self-image. Remember self-belief and the importance of seeing yourself in the right way? This comes back to your thoughts.

There are all kinds of people out there and each has their own way of interpreting and processing life. When it comes to thoughts, people have different ways of producing them. Some people literally just have a thought about something. Others are more feeling based and will feel an emotion first, followed by a certain thought – perhaps of a person or situation, maybe a task that needs doing, or the thought of a memory. Others have thoughts but understand them as a "voice" in their heads, which they can hear speak internally. All of these are different ways of thinking and there are probably many more ways used by some of the 7 billion+ people on this planet right now.

It doesn't matter how your thoughts come up, what matters is there are similarities between all people in some ways. One of these is how we can have "intrusive" thoughts. An intrusive thought is one that comes out without you actively choosing to think about it. It happens to everyone, but these thoughts can be more frequent and more intense in some people than others.

To overcome these, most people start resisting the thoughts or trying to distract themselves by focusing elsewhere. This isn't a good choice because the more you resist the thought, the more power you give it. Meditation can be a great way to learn about this process, because when we meditate we are aiming to become aware of everything around us without being overly attached.

Meditation teaches you to be in the moment and to hear the sounds around you, feel the air temperature, the feel of the chair you're sitting on, and smell the scents that are around you. The reason we are taught not to label or linger on any of this when we meditate is because lingering on something, naming/labelling it, or even trying to focus on it more intensely will bring you out of the moment. It will create a focus on a thing, which you have defined in your mind, which you have expectations from. Instead, just enjoy the experience without any assumptions or expectations.

When you can do this with the sounds and smells around you, you can also do it with thoughts and emotions. Sometimes you will feel an emotion or a thought will suddenly pop into your head. **Do not resist it!** There's a reason for every thought or emotion we experience. The reason is often related to the way we are hard-wired. Yes, once again those evolutionary traits that have helped us for so long might now be holding you back.

You know that by being aware of your instincts and why they are happening, you can lessen their power over you. The same is true of your thoughts. If you can become aware of them and observe them *without* getting attached or caught up in them, then they will lose their power over you. Meditation teaches you to do exactly that; it teaches you to let your thoughts pass and acknowledge them without attaching yourself to the experience.

Once more, I would urge you to check out one of our meditation or mindfulness guides to gain a deeper understanding of how to do this.

When you first start meditating, just separating from your thoughts is the main focus. Beginners will get lost in the thought, they will be distracted by it and give it focus. At some point, they will realize that they aren't in the moment anymore, instead having gotten caught up in the thought. This is where the thought can be acknowledged and let go.

Over time it becomes easier to let thoughts go, and you can reach the point where a thought drifts through your mind without any attachment, allowing you to accept it and let it go before it can gain a foothold in your mind. This is the stage where you are observing your thoughts instead of experiencing them from within. You have separated your awareness and life energy from your thought process. The brain is an organ just like any other in the body, it is not YOU, it is an organ that serves you and is powered by you.

Observation of your thoughts gives you a deeper understanding of where they come from and why they are happening. You'll get an understanding of the reasons behind the way you think and why specific thoughts seem to come into your mind by themselves. This is another level of knowing yourself, another level of delving into your inner workings.

As your understanding of the *why* behind your thoughts begins to grow, you will get some important answers. You'll know what it is that your evolutionary hard-wiring is trying to avoid. You'll know if it's a fear of risk or exposure, or if it's a fear of failure. You'll know if there are past events that somehow keep on surfacing and affecting you. You'll know if there is some underlying anxiety or fear powering your thoughts.

It isn't all negative answers though. Understanding your thoughts and the reasons they occur can also show you what you really desire and what makes you feel good or at home. You can figure out the best ways to motivate yourself and what you desire. Using this information you can create a frame (or scenario) for your life, which integrates your wants, needs, and desires with the work you need to do to achieve your goals. It's an even deeper level of understanding that pleasure will come in the long-term by doing what's needed now. It's having that same understanding when it comes to putting off work and being undisciplined, and how allowing these things to happen will cause you long-term pain in your life.

It's not magic, but it will feel that way once you get the hang of it. Understanding yourself means you can align your life in a harmonious way so that everything has a purpose and a goal and that all of those reasons are totally understood by you at all times. When you know why you're doing what you're doing and have faith in the payoff, you are much more likely to stay on the path to success and stay disciplined.

Your evolutionary hard-wiring will begin to accept that the better path is to let you take active control, as it realizes the pain of staying disciplined is minor while the reward is major. It will stop fighting against you, letting you easily reach a more productive state.

More than that, you'll start to have less and less intrusive thoughts. Your mind will wander less and your focus will improve. There are a whole bunch of other positive effects to regular meditation as well, such as a better immune system and less stress (proven by lower levels of cortisol in the body). Remember what we said about thoughts becoming words and actions? At this stage, you will have incredible control over your thoughts, eliminating any negative or intrusive ones. That allows you to live without any negativity in your mind, which means your words and actions are much more likely to be positive.

Positive momentum starts here, with your thoughts. Carry it through each day and you will find yourself becoming more disciplined, more productive, and more motivated. By mastering control over your own mind, you have virtually taken control of your reality.

CHAPTER 9: EMOTIONS, FEAR, AND SETBACKS

Thoughts are a difficult area to control, but we've already covered the best way to do it. The methods in this guide will work for anybody if they are used in the way instructed, which means anybody can gain control over their own thoughts. Anybody can shape their mental state from here and create the life they want.

Imagine now that you've progressed far enough that your thoughts are under control and you're beginning to see success in all areas of your life. Suddenly disaster strikes – some kind of crisis involving your work and professional life. Now you're under massive amounts of stress from out of nowhere, and yet it's more important than ever that you stay totally functional and productive. It's more important than ever that you stay calm and clear headed so that you can make the right decisions.

While all of this is going on, you've also had something bad happen in your personal life. It could be something truly terrible, such as a loved one falling seriously ill or being hurt badly. There's even more pressure on you and to make matters worse, your mind is constantly focused on your family instead of what you need to do at work.

With the pressure on and emotions high, it's easy for your mood to fall and for you to feel lower than usual. If this happens, your self-discipline in life will be tested. Many people struggle to keep their discipline up in the face of tough times. Excuses start to pop into our minds and we start to believe that these reasons to back off are real. How could you keep on being positive and productive during such a bad time?

THE IMPORTANCE OF RESILIENCE

Life is a roller coaster journey full of ups and downs. A few chapters ago we touched on a former Navy SEAL named David Goggins. This man is known for his mental toughness, discipline, and his incredible resilience. Goggins is a former world record holder for the most pull-ups done in 24 hours. During his first attempt at this record in 2012, he pushed so hard that a muscle actually burst through the skin of his right arm. A later x-ray confirmed the muscle itself had also torn.

Despite this setback and the immense pain it would have caused him, David was back at a pull-up bar and about to try and break the record once more after just two months. Once again he started off with a great pace and was well over half way to the record in the first 12 hours. Once again he suffered an injury, this time to his left hand, which derailed him and stopped the attempt.

After two horrific injuries within two months, most people would have given up altogether. Goggins waited only another two months, taking us to January 2013. This time he managed to set a new world record (at the time) with 4,030 pull-ups within 24 hours.

David Goggins is an example of toughness and resilience. He is a man who refuses to accept defeat with his mind. He also refuses to accept negative emotions or weakness in the face of adversity. For him there wasn't much of a choice. He had to be mentally and emotionally strong just to survive the childhood he lived through.

Goggins was a victim of extreme abuse as a child. He spent the early years of his life attending school during the day and working at his father's skating rink after school. The long gruelling hours left him exhausted and unable to perform at school. During all of this, David would witness the physical abuse his mother endured at the hands of his father. David's father would also target him sometimes, whether with a belt or a hand.

After escaping his father at the age of eight, David had to experience the hardship of being separated from his older brother. On top of that, he ended up moving to an almost exclusively white area. This area also happened to be a hub for the KKK, so you can imagine that Goggins experienced a huge amount of racism at school. His teachers didn't care and neither did anybody else. He was the only black child there, so they ignored his complaints and left him to be victimised by the other students.

David also began to experience severe learning difficulties as a result of the stress from his childhood. Even at such a young age, he began to lose hair and developed a stutter. His life as a victim continued with the racism now affecting him out of school as well. As if all of this wasn't enough, his father refused to give any decent amount of cash for him or his mother to live on. They survived in poverty conditions, living in squalor and going without any of the extras in life.

A lot of people in the world would have broken and folded at even one of these terrible events. For David, they didn't even stop there. He ended up reaching adulthood and deciding to join the military, dreaming that one day he could be a pararescue soldier. Here his emotions were tested again as he had to learn how to swim. David had never been able to afford swimming lessons, and he was extremely fearful of the water.

During medical tests at this point, it was revealed that he had a vulnerability to sickle cell anemia. Suffering mentally and emotionally from the hardships of his life, Goggins made the choice to fold and leave the military. The sickle cell trait was his reason, a genuine excuse to get out of the military and to abandon his dreams of being part of an elite unit.

If asked about these days, Goggins is fast to admit that he was choosing the easy way out. He admits that he could have stayed, could have pushed harder, and maybe even made it to his dream of being a paratrooper. The real reason he left wasn't the medical diagnosis, it was the increasing fear and discomfort he was feeling because of the swimming tests and challenges.

Falling into one of the lowest times in his life, Goggins began to put on weight rapidly. He became obese and unhealthy, now working a low-rate job as an exterminator. Still suffering from his past, still experiencing racism, and feeling at one of the lowest points of his life, David Goggins stumbled across something that lit a fire in him – a documentary on the Navy SEALs.

Here was a group of people who formed one of the world's most elite fighting forces. This brotherhood could go to hell and back without cracking or folding. They could endure the toughest of situations and keep on ticking. At this time, one thing David KNEW was that something had to change. He had to push hard one more time to find what was within him because he was entirely sick and tired of his mediocre existence. He **refused** to stay at this low point. Instead, he decided then and there to go through whatever it would take in order to reach his goals and become the person he wanted to be.

Having already suffered in bits and pieces through life, Goggins decided he was going to suffer willingly, and professionally, in extreme ways. He would suck it up and absorb whatever hell was inflicted on him during BUD/S camp and the rest of Navy SEAL training. He would endure this pain because he knew it was temporary. He knew that by going through this hell, he would be able to escape the hell he was already living in every day. He knew that by enduring the short-term pain of becoming a SEAL, he would defeat the long-term pain of his unhappy life. This is a real life example of **emotional resilience**, a man who went through unspeakable pain and came out on the other side refusing to be broken.

If you want to succeed in life and be truly disciplined, you need to be resilient too. Life will throw you a curveball at some point; it will come up with a situation that messes with you on an emotional level. Something could happen to a loved one, or your relationship could fall apart suddenly. Disasters happen all over the world each and every day, and none of us are safe from their effects.

When these things happen, the worst thing you can do is respond emotionally. You must remain calm and remain focused on your goals.

DEALING WITH EMOTIONAL REACTIONS

Emotions and thoughts can both pop up unexpectedly and derail your discipline. Thoughts can pop up because of underlying fears or insecurities. You might also get intrusive thoughts, which seem to happen without any reason – they just seem to pop up at unrelated times by themselves.

You've learned already how to get past these thoughts – simply be aware of them and acknowledge them. Resisting them gives them more power and drains some of your willpower, leaving you with less for anything else you need to do. Allowing them and then observing them keeps your willpower free for other things. If you can allow the thought and observe it as if you were an outsider, it loses its power. You can look at the thought logically and might see that it actually seems like a silly thing to worry about. Other times you will figure out what your deeper fears are by observing thoughts and be able to calm your mind by reminding it that logically, you are in no real danger.

Emotions work in a similar way too, but not exactly the same. Emotions usually happen as a reaction to some kind of event, so they aren't as random as thoughts. It is possible to randomly feel emotions at times, but this is usually a sign of something else being wrong – usually there are strong emotions being repressed and held back. By burying emotions deep down and ignoring them, we create a big problem for ourselves.

The human body has to be healthy and happy to operate properly. If you are hiding massive stress and emotional trauma, it can begin to surface in other ways. David Goggins suffered from toxic stress as a child, causing him to lose hair and skin pigment while developing a stutter. He also suffered with learning difficulties, another symptom of toxic stress. All of this happened because he was undergoing emotional trauma with no healthy way to process it or understand it. Fortunately, he survived this rough childhood and went on to become one of the strongest people in existence.

The problem that humans have with emotions is that we don't like the unpleasant ones. We try to avoid them because we don't want to feel bad, or angry, or sad. Sometimes we are able to bury them for a while without any major bad signs coming up, but that doesn't always work. The other problem with burying emotions is the more you bury, the harder it becomes to keep everything hidden. As more and more emotional baggage builds up inside you, your ability to deal with new emotional trauma becomes smaller and smaller.

Eventually something might burst back out unexpectedly, leading to a panic attack or breakdown. For some people, this starts an outpouring of emotion and trauma as everything that was buried all comes tumbling out at the same time. In this state, people can shut down entirely. I've heard plenty of stories about soldiers in warzones who suddenly broke down. Some of them freak out and shut down entirely, unable to continue fighting, doing nothing but hiding and trying to survive. Others go into the depths of despair, accepting death and remembering all of the terror that they have seen, while some go in the opposite direction and become hysterical, laughing uncontrollably and believing nothing can hurt them – or even that none of this is real.

It doesn't matter which way somebody cracks, what matters is that they cracked in the first place – and a big part of it was those buried emotions, which become fuel for the breakdown.

To deal with emotions, you first **have to experience them**. This is a bit different from allowing a thought, because with an emotion you are going to feel it fully when you experience it – this is why some people initially bury the emotion. There are times when burying the emotion is the right thing to do. If you're in the middle of an important meeting and you get some bad news, you may have to bury that until the meeting is finished. A soldier in the field might have to experience the death of his friends around him and have to bury it until the mission is over – there is no time in the field to stop or mourn. These are examples of how burying an emotion can be a good thing, but it should only be done temporarily and if it's REALLY needed.

The emotion still needs to be felt and processed though, and this should happen as soon as there is time and space for it. Experiencing emotions in this way, especially negative ones, can be very hard. If you avoid it though, the negative emotion will be leaking into your life and affecting you for the rest of your time on this earth. It's better to just experience the emotion now, fully and intensely. It will feel bad at times; it will feel upsetting and might make you feel angry at the world. There's a reason you feel this way though; allow it and experience it. It isn't wrong to be angry over injustices in your life. It isn't wrong to be sad when something bad happens or to wonder how life could be so cruel in the first place.

When you experience your emotions in this way, the feeling will gradually begin to pass. You don't have to make sense of what happened – sometimes things happen for no reason, and bad things can happen to good people just like good things can happen to bad people. There is no ruleset to the world or any real reason for anything to happen. Life is quite random in that way.

Emotions can take a lot longer to work through than thoughts. Thoughts can be dealt with in minutes. Emotions can sometimes be dealt with in minutes too. Other times they might need hours, days, or even weeks. It all depends on the level of the feeling and what caused it.

Along with life events, some people will also experience emotions at random times – sudden anxiety or fear are good examples. This is usually related to burying emotions and not dealing with them or not being aware of your own emotional state. Meditation is helpful here, too, because it calms you enough to notice when you're entering an emotional state.

In those situations, it's the deeper trauma that you need to find and understand. You have to figure out what you have buried and why. Then you can begin to unlock that feeling inside you and process the emotional trauma there.

Whether the emotion is caused by something new or something already there, you still have to feel it to process it. When you allow an emotion to be felt, it begins to lose its intensity over time. Some emotions are strong enough that you might never totally process and release it, like if a loved one has passed away. That's okay; you don't need every emotion to leave you completely.

Process the ones that can be processed and let them go. Understand the feelings you're having and accept them as justified. Then you can release the emotion and carry on with your life. Learning to deal with emotions in this way makes it harder for you to be emotionally affected in the future too. Once you become really good at processing emotions, most events won't have any noticeable effect on you. You'll be able to ignore emotions healthily in the short-term and process them in the long-term.

EMOTIONAL FUEL

For more intense emotions (such as the death example), we are going to struggle to completely let go. This is when you process the feeling until it loses most of its intensity. In the case of a death, you would process it to the point where you can actually function in the world again. It may be years until you totally accept this person has gone, and that isn't a bad thing.

Emotions that last a lot longer can be used in a different way though. They can be processed enough that they don't cause us any damage, and then they can be used as fuel for your discipline.

With negative emotions and events, you might be left with some anger or rage. You can choose to channel this and use it as fuel for your discipline. I've heard many military personnel talk about how they have pushed so far in life because they are driven by the memories of their friends who are no longer here. Because they have close people who aren't even alive anymore, they use it as their reason to live as fully as possible and to achieve the most they possibly can. There are others who have incredible drive fuelled by the deaths of family members, particularly parents. These people are doing everything possible to make their loved ones proud, whether they're still here or not.

Doing this with a raw emotion is dangerous because it can fuel you in erratic ways. It can lead you to taking extreme actions that are dangerous and unnecessary. It's better to process the feeling as much as you can. Personally, I use this method myself, because my life has had some bad events too. Like many other people, I have experienced bad times and have lost some family members unexpectedly. I managed to process my emotions until I was past the depression stage and past feeling angry at the entire world. I processed them until I was able to be functional, but still I felt a slow burning anger within over the things that had happened.

It's this slow burning anger that I look for anytime I feel tired, lazy, or overwhelmed. It reminds me that there are people I wish could be here today to experience life with me –

and it reminds me that those people aren't able to experience anything anymore. That drives me to do everything in my power and leave a mark in their honour. It drives me to achieve all that I can so when my time comes, my loved ones can live a little easier than I did, and so they can feel proud of all I did before leaving this existence.

Positive emotions can work in the same way too. Visualizing the life you want to live and the happiness you could feel. If you have a partner, you might imagine the rewards you will both get thanks to your discipline. You might think of the extra time you guys could have together if you achieve financial freedom through mental discipline.

This also works for positive experiences that you've had in the past. You can mentally associate your continued mental discipline with the reward of positive experiences. You can use them as a goal/target to aim for when pushing through your daily tasks. A combination of positive emotions and negative emotions can create super-high drive. For some people, positive works better, while for others it's negative. Combining both can supercharge your fuel tank though and give you some real, intense reasons to want to continue and reach your goals.

If you can make a goal feel very personal and closely associated to the negative (or positive) events in your life, then it gives you a lot more reason to stay disciplined. When something happens that affects you deeply, it's hard to entirely let go. You can process and accept it, but you probably won't forget it. Remember earlier when I talked about my own negative feelings and how I use them as fuel? You can do the same.

If you have experienced discomfort, stress, or hard times in life, *use them* to fuel your journey. Use that feeling of being teased to fuel your drive for a new body. Use the horrible things you've been through to provide determination for success, so if something happens again, you're at least much more prepared for it. Some of us are bothered daily by things in our past. That's okay, just use it in a good way, as something to drive you towards success.

Emotional Toughness

Experiencing emotions and allowing them to be felt in full is a good thing for one other reason too – it desensitizes you. When people bury their emotions immediately, they never really feel them. They decide the pain/hurt is too much and bury the feeling, ignoring it completely. If you choose to go through these feelings and experience them instead, the negative feelings will have less effect on you next time. You toughen yourself and become more able to deal with bad situations.

Emotional toughness isn't about denying feelings, it's about allowing them so you can build up some resistance and resilience. Thoughts are a lot easier to deal with because they come from the logical part of your body – the brain. They usually make sense and it's easier to analyze them and pick them apart. When you've figured out the reasons for them and how to deal with them, it's quite straightforward.

Emotions don't work that way. They come from the way you feel, which isn't so logical. Usually they originate from outside of your body, too, from a place you can't control. Life is full of random events and some of those are always going to be bad. Remember that life is a roller coaster; it has as many downs as ups. Without the bad experiences, you wouldn't be able to feel happiness anyway.

Think of a child who is raised in a sheltered and privileged life. They almost never experience anything bad. At some point, say in their teen years, they experience a bad social rejection or a break-up. This would be a massive feeling of pain and loss compared to anything they've felt before. They would be feeling a huge amount of trauma.

Compare that to a child from a third world country who has grown up surrounded by war. If this child makes it to a safer place by their teen years, then experiences the same break-up, they won't be so badly affected. They'll have experienced many worse lows than this already and can probably shrug off the break-up and process it healthily. For this person, joy can be reached a lot easier too. Just being safe in everyday life and having access to food, water, clothing, and shelter would be a massive bonus to this person.

The spoiled child from the first example wouldn't really value those things though. They'd already be used to the basics in life and could even take the luxuries for granted.

The point is that everybody has an emotional "level" based on their life experiences. Understanding this can help you to process any negative emotions that come your way. In the second part, we will look at a psychological technique called "framing," which can help a lot with this too.

Building emotional toughness just comes down to accepting anything bad that does happen and working through it. It helps to remember that no matter what terrible situation happens, there are other people who have been through it and survived, even thrived. There are also plenty of people out there who are in worse circumstances and who aren't giving up. The world is full of many horrors, and compared to some of them, our lives really aren't that bad.

We always have to accept what has happened, has happened, whether it was good or bad. From there, we have to process it and live with it. If we can use these emotions for fuel, they can be turned to our advantage, but with some of the bad ones (like the sorrow of losing someone), we will still feel a pain or sorrow attached to what happened.

This usually happens when we are struggling to figure out the reason why. Why would something so bad happen? Why to you or somebody you care so much for? The simple answer is – there is no known and obvious reason. Life doesn't give us straight answers. The best we can do is live with the intention of creating positivity and not hurting others.

Emotions might hurt, but they don't have to control you, and you don't have to let them dictate your life and your outcome. You can still be sad and disciplined at the same time. Emotional toughness is about showing life that it won't turn you from what you really want – even if you happen to encounter pain along that journey. The person who can make any worthwhile life journey without experiencing pain is rare indeed. What matters more is the person who can take it in their stride and keep moving, even if they need a small break or to slow down for a little while. Never leave the path entirely though. Rest when you must, then remember your reasons for being disciplined and get back on the path.

CHAPTER 10: OVERCOMING FEARS AND SETBACKS

When it comes to discipline, a big part of it is figuring out what is stopping you and why. Some of the biggest problems that people have with mental discipline are caused by their own minds and the thoughts they give out.

Intrusive thoughts, negative thinking, and a lack of self-belief are all problems rooted in your thoughts. Your thoughts aren't the cause of them though. The cause is some kind of fear, doubt, or lack of confidence. These problems cause you to doubt yourself or your ability. It won't even be clear that this is why the thoughts are coming up, and your reasons will be different from other people's reasons.

In my case, the fear was that I wasn't good enough to accomplish what I wanted to. I was working hard already and trying to get ahead, but I noticed that I kept handicapping myself. My discipline would be lacking at the worst possible times, so I was always doing everything at the last minute, cramming things in, and rushing around.

This was when I started getting deeper into **self-analysis**. I wanted to figure out what was *really* happening below the surface, because on the surface, I fully wanted to be successful and I totally intended to be on top of everything. From research I learned there are some common fears that people have that hold them back in life. You ever feel like you really want to do something, or even *need* to do something, but it just seems so hard to actually get started? Ever have plenty of time to get work done, only to find yourself going at a slow pace, not really concentrating or trying, until it's almost too late? It feels weird, almost like you don't really have control over yourself. The problem is we have underlying fears, and those are holding us back in some way. It's usually hard to see what the fear is or why it's hindering us because that's a deep-wired thing, powered by the darkest corners of your mind and emotions, plus evolutionary habits.

Plenty of people have caught on to this pattern though, and some of them have investigated it intensely. They've been able to break deep into the human psyche and find the process and beliefs behind these fears. By doing that, they've discovered which fears are common amongst most people.

COMMON CAUSES OF SELF-SABOTAGE

I've listed the biggest fears here for you, along with the reasoning your body/mind/soul applies to them. Remember it's this reasoning, this perception, that causes the problems and not the fear itself.

Logic can defeat these pre-made perceptions. With logic, you can see these feelings are grounded in negativity and doubt, not facts. Note - this list doesn't cover the fear of every human alive; there are always going to be some people who are just wired differently. Here are the common deep fears that humans tend to have:

- Fear of Change – Succeeding could mean change. Even trying to succeed could mean change. Change is seen as stressful, potentially bad, and a hard thing to go through. And who knows what it will actually change into!? Maybe it's better to stick with the life you know.

- Fear of Responsibility – If you do start to succeed in life, you might be handed more responsibilities. You could end up having to make much more important decisions or be responsible for other people. That's a stressful place to be, especially if you make a mistake! Maybe it's better to avoid all of that and just be responsible for yourself.

- Fear of Expectation/Pressure – Sometimes when you start to succeed or do well, people expect you to keep that up. What if you can't? Your mind might even like the idea of being successful and great at something, but the idea of keeping that level up for the rest of your life sounds long, daunting, and tiring. After all, it can feel like success is fleeting. Once you reach a mark, you just make a newer one and have to start the process all over again. Maybe it's easier to just avoid all of that and stay in a safe, quiet position. That way nobody can expect anything from you, right?

- Fear of Being Inadequate – This is usually a socially fuelled fear. It's a fear of looking bad in front of others if you fail or of finding out yourself that you aren't as good as you thought. The thing is, everybody fails sometimes. It's natural to be bad at something, that's why we have to learn and gain experience. Over time, you start to get better, and you can succeed. If you fear failure in the first place, maybe because you feel you'll be ridiculed or something, then it's pretty hard to get going at all. In this case, you're associating failure with so much pain that you'd rather just not try – Maybe it's safer to not try, because that way you can't possibly be embarrassed.

- Fear of Attention – Some people don't actually want to be the center of attention. They don't want to stand out. There are sayings like "the tallest blade of grass gets cut first" and "the nail which sticks out gets hammered." These sayings relate to this fear; they're suggesting that if you stand out too much, you're going to be targeted. That can happen, but the chances of reaching this level are slim. Let's face it, not many people are going to be the Steve Jobs and Elon Musks of this world. For most of us, we don't need to be. We can fulfil all of our dreams without being one of the few most known people in a population of well over 7 billion. That's why this fear is ridiculous. If you don't want attention, there's plenty of ways to avoid it. You can be successful and as much of a grey man or woman as you like. Maybe it is better to just not try, maybe being nobody at all is better than risking a slight chance of some uncomfortable attention, right?

- Fear of Ridicule – This one is similar to the fears of attention and pressure. I'm sure that you've seen a comedian get heckled by the crowd at some point. You might have even seen a performer or speaker of some type get booed offstage. These things happen sometimes in life, but it isn't the end of the world. It's just a sign that something has to change, and you need to adapt. Unfortunately, some people are so afraid of being told they're not good enough that they won't try in the first place. Maybe it's better to give up on your dreams if reaching them means you have to hear some nasty words.

- Fear of Ego – Some people are worried about success because they think it will change them. This comes from a lack of trust in themselves. Of course, if you were handed unlimited money and power right now, it could easily corrupt you over time. When you have to earn it and fight for it, you tend to appreciate it a lot more. There's a reason that the people with the most responsibility also have the most power – they're the ones who are able to make the right decisions. If they weren't, they wouldn't have reached that position in the first place. This is true for you as well. The journey to your destination is going to teach and change you, but not in a bad way. This is called personal growth and everybody should be looking to grow. Avoiding success because you don't want to change is like a child avoiding growing up because they don't want themselves or their lives to change. It's great that you feel happy with the way you are now and your life at the moment, but change and growth are much more likely to make it (and you) better than worse. Maybe the possibility of misusing power is reason enough to avoid your life goals and avoid achieving anything though.

- Fear of Workload – This one is a bit more logical than the others. It's rooted in a lack of self-belief, which then means there's not much belief in the journey ending and actually having a pay-off. It happens when you're already making sacrifices to try and succeed in life, and they're costing you in other areas, like your social or family life. If you succeed, the workload is going to get heavier and restrict your time even more, right? Not really. Unless you DO want to be Elon or Branson, you're probably going to reach a level where you're happy and start focusing on making life more pleasant instead of pushing for more and more career success. You know your goals and what you need to live a happy life. Once you achieve it, there's no reason for you to be locked in and sacrificing your time. In fact, it frees your time up – that's the reason most people WANT to succeed! But hey – maybe it's better to have a little free time now and sacrifice the possibility of an early retirement and loads of free time later.

- Fear of Social Change – A bit like the fear of ego, this is a fear that success will change your life. This time it isn't about trusting yourself and abusing power, it's about the other people in your life. This fear is often rooted in a feeling of disconnection or separation from others. You feel cut off so you feel like you will be making this journey alone – and then others will be left behind. The truth is you're always going to have people come in and out of your life, so some people will get left behind whether you change or not. By pushing yourself though, you can be in a position to help those around you. You also act as inspiration for them and can pass on the knowledge on how to succeed. This is good for the people in your life! Being successful is never going to have a bad impact on people around you unless they don't care about your well-being. In that case, it's better to find out and get rid of these people anyway. Unless, maybe it's better to not achieve anything. Maybe then people will feel sorry for you and be sympathetic, paying attention to you despite the fact that you have nothing to offer?

- Fear of Disappointment – Sometimes the fear is of actually succeeding and getting what you want. The fear is that it won't live up to your expectations and that you still won't be happy – it won't have made any real difference to how you feel. It's like the whole "money doesn't make you happy" saying but applied to all areas of your success. Of course money can't buy you happiness, but it *can* buy you a lot of freedom to live the life you want instead of the life you have to. It can also give you a lot of options that aren't available otherwise. Why would you not want these benefits? It goes beyond money, too, because success comes in many forms, and they are all worthwhile. This fear comes from a lack of faith, but it's an easier one to overcome with logic. You just analyze the situation and reassure your brain that you are taking the best course of action. Unless, maybe it's better to just not ever try and never know or have any idea how happy you *could* have been.

SETBACKS

Fears aren't the only obstacle on the path to success. There are going to be setbacks sometimes, not everything goes to plan. Sometimes the plan has to change, and a setback is nothing more than a sign to push you in the right direction. This is easier to deal with when the setback is work related, but sometimes setbacks come from other sources. Sometimes the problem is with your health, love life, or elsewhere. Life is always going to give you random problems from time to time.

If you let it, these problems can derail you. It's easy to slip into a negative mindset or emotional state when something bad happens. For these situations, you have to rely on what you learned earlier about mental and emotional toughness. You have to be able to accept a situation and look at it objectively. You also have to experience the negative emotions so they can no longer take hold on you. Remain in the moment and always keep your true focus in mind.

Setbacks are nothing more than hurdles on your race to your dreams. You have to overcome them if you want to reach the destination. They're the reason that most people aren't willing to go the full distance and will fall off before you. Remember your positive self-image – you are a doer and you make your own luck. Shrug off any setbacks (as much as possible) and keep on moving forwards.

PART 2

We've gone over thoughts and how to control them, which is a great way to hone your mind. We've also covered the importance of emotions and dealing with hard times in life. These are both areas that you have to get control of to maintain discipline. Self-belief and an analytical approach are the bases that launch your discipline, with willpower being the fuel. Careful planning aids your navigation through the realm of mental discipline. This completes the "blueprint."

In this second part, we are going to look at more practical tips for improving and maintaining your mental discipline.

CHAPTER 11: HOW TO MAXIMIZE YOUR WILLPOWER

Back in the first part, we covered some basic facts on willpower. An important one is that you have a limited amount of willpower, so you must use it wisely. Another is that you can shortcut it a little by creating habits. You can also increase the amount you have, which we will look at in more detail now, and it can be affected by momentum – both good and bad.

COGNITIVE FATIGUE AND THE WILLPOWER GAUGE

Cognitive fatigue is tiredness of the mind. Your brain is like the other muscles in your body, it gets tired as it's used. As you go through the day, you need to pay attention to lots of different things. There's a lot to think about, to observe, and to take in, whether it's from work or your personal life. All of this wears down your mind, tiring it out. This is why people find it harder to learn late in the day – a lot of your brains energy has been used up already. After intense exercise, people are less capable of doing mental tasks, too, because the low energy levels and general tiredness also affects your brain.

I've seen the effects of this first hand when observing fighters training. Early in training sessions, fighters are very mentally capable. They can take on new combinations and movements, drilling them on the pads. I've also watched some fight camp sessions, where these people do gruelling physical workouts. At the end of these sessions, the coach might do some simple combination work. The idea is to train when tired, mentally and physically. By doing this, the moves become ingrained in the memory, because they are now being performed without much thought. However, because mental energy is so low, the simple combinations are hard to pick up and plenty of fighters will make mistakes doing really simple moves.

This is an example of cognitive fatigue. Remembering a sequence of four moves has become difficult for the type of athlete that regularly pulls off new 8-10 move combos when fresh. Cognitive fatigue affects your ability to analyze a situation or any information. It affects the way you see problems and the solutions you can come up with. It also affects your decision-making abilities, with tired people making worse decisions than they normally would.

To stay disciplined, it's best to be mentally fresh, avoiding this cognitive fatigue, so that you don't end up making bad decisions. The problem it that cognitive fatigue is hard to avoid. It's like telling an athlete that they need to stay fresh to perform at their best – performing at their best is going to be tiring, so obviously they can't stay fresh!

Decision fatigue is an idea that is related to cognitive fatigue. Under this theory, every decision you make through the day takes away some of your decision-making fuel. Even simple decisions like where to eat, what to wear, or what order to do your tasks in – they all cost you some decision making fuel. Decision fatigue is related to cognitive fatigue too. Suffering from cognitive fatigue affects your decisions, and having to make enough decisions eventually leads to cognitive fatigue.

We already talked before about the willpower gauge as well and how you have a limited amount each day. There's a big relation between cognitive fatigue, decision fatigue, and the willpower gauge. Running low on one seems to affect the others heavily. If you show signs of cognitive fatigue, it's pretty tough to keep making good decisions, and it's hard to show any willpower too.

Signs of cognitive fatigue (or mental fatigue) include confusion, mood swings, and lack of motivation. These are only some of the bad symptoms, but for matters involving mental discipline, they're the worst. Cognitive fatigue will sap you of your will to push on and make everything seem a bit harder.

Trying to stay disciplined in the face of an empty willpower gauge and no mental energy is almost impossible. Dealing with this has a few approaches. The first is to increase the size of your willpower gauge. This part has been covered already, but we'll recap it in a moment. The other two techniques you can use are willpower management, so that your willpower lasts for longer, and recharging techniques, which can help top up your gauge temporarily.

INCREASING OVERALL WILLPOWER AND MENTAL CAPACITY

Boosting your overall willpower is a gradual process. Like with other parts of the human body, willpower is increased by using it regularly. As you begin to practice daily discipline, your amount of willpower will naturally grow. Living a generally healthy lifestyle is also helpful to boosting willpower.

Let's use diet as an example. If you have bad dietary habits, they can affect your willpower. Let me show you how. First let's say you don't have a routine for your food – meaning you don't think much about what you eat OR when you eat. Now you have to make an active decision on when to eat and what to eat. This is two decisions made, both draining your decision-making ability a little. Decision making and cognitive fatigue both seem related to willpower, but it's possible to still have some willpower even when you're a bit burned out on the mental side and decision making.

So with two decisions, you give the willpower tank a slight hit too. If you've given in to temptation with your food choices, this also gives your momentum a hit, making it more likely that you'll make bad decisions afterwards too. Because you don't have a schedule, you might get back to work a bit late, too, and take it a bit slower – both bad decisions and both further tanking your willpower.

On the flipside, we have the person who eats on time and has a schedule for it – it doesn't have to be to the minute, just accurate enough that they know when to eat and when to get back to work. With the decision already made on what to eat, there's less thought involved, preserving the willpower. Having these types of routines and good habits builds positive momentum for your day. It also gets your mind used to making the right decision with less thought, so less willpower is needed for each choice. Over time, you get used to living this way, and it becomes easy to stick to your original choices. Discipline is taking effect, your willpower is growing, and what used to seem hard now seems routine.

Eating healthy, whole foods also helps keep your body healthy and stable. Making sure you don't experience sugar crashes, cravings, and other negative states is important. Your body needs a good supply of vitamins and minerals to stay healthy, too, and a good supply of clean energy. Provide it with all of this in your diet to keep your body and mind functioning at their best. This way it becomes easier to stay disciplined.

The use of a healthy diet will make you feel better in general and is helpful for discipline. A happy, healthy person has much more willpower than an unhealthy one because they have a better mood, more focus, and more energy.

Meditation and mindfulness link back to willpower in the same way. Discipline feels more difficult when energy levels are low. Likewise, if a person feels unwell or tired, they will find it harder to stay disciplined. Everything you do throughout the day uses some mental energy. Every thought you have, including the intrusive ones that happen themselves, all have a cost. Every action you take, every feeling you experience, they can all cost you a little willpower. Mindfulness is a way to take back control over your thoughts and lessen the impact of negative or intrusive thoughts. Over time you will start to get less of those thoughts, and each one will have less impact on you anyway.

Your emotional state will also become more balanced, and the proven drop in cortisol only has positive effects on your body. It's like the start of a positive spiral that hits all of the areas mentioned here. Better diet and mindfulness can both improve your health and willpower, making it easier to make good choices, which then help you to live a better, healthier life – again making you more disciplined, and again leading to more good choices and habits.

Exercise is another great way to boost your overall willpower. First, there are plenty of general health benefits to exercise, and second, it's a great stress reducer. This general boost to your health will help your willpower. By burning some energy with focused exercise, you also stop yourself from feeling restless if you need to spend large parts of the day sitting around. This is helpful for your focus and can also help you to relax, plus it will help you to sleep better – more on that later.

Many training types keep you mentally sharp, too, without requiring too much mental effort. Over time, your day-to-day energy levels will increase and your mood can also be positively altered.

Intense exercise gets you used to working in tough conditions. This is a great way to increase willpower and is a method used by special forces units all over the world. The selection process for every unit I've heard of involves extreme physical testing for long time periods. It isn't really about whether they're fit enough, because nobody will ever be fit enough to breeze through these tests. They're designed to take everybody to their limit and keep them there, where they feel exhausted, stressed, and hurt at all times. To survive, they have to weather the mental storm and keep pushing. It doesn't matter how fit they are, what matters is that they never quit. This develops extreme mental discipline and makes them trainable – people who can be transformed into the ultimate combat machines, true warrior athletes. It all comes from their discipline, and their discipline is proven and built by physical struggle.

It's unreasonable and unrealistic for anybody to put themselves through this, but by pushing through difficulty in the physical world, you can build a bigger discipline tank on the mental side.

WILLPOWER MANAGEMENT

Growing your overall willpower is a gradual process, which sees small improvements over time. Another way to make more of what you have already is to learn how to manage it. Let's pretend that your willpower tank is the same as a cars fuel tank. So far we've been focusing on getting a bigger tank so we have more fuel. What if we also made the engine more efficient though? That way the same size tank would get the car further along its journey.

A lot of life is about making the most of what you already have. For example, everybody has their own individual talents. We all have strengths and weaknesses, areas that we enjoy and those that we dislike. There aren't many characteristics in common amongst successful people either – not when it comes to talents at least. They all have certain things in common like a high drive, the ability to motivate themselves, discipline to get things done, high work rate, etc. These are all traits that can be modelled and learned though, they aren't natural strengths or weaknesses.

When it comes to natural attributes, successful people are those who make the most out of them. One person might be a genius with numbers and leverage that strength to get what they want out of life. Another might be an athletic beast, using hard work to become a professional athlete on the back of that talent. Another might be a great people person and focus on creating teams and businesses based on that skill.

Life is about working with what you have and leveraging it. Richard Branson is another example who comes to mind. Branson is the founder and owner of the Virgin brand. These days he is known as a successful entrepreneur and billionaire, but there was a time when Richard Branson was a dyslexic teenager, struggling in school. Dropping out of school at

15, Branson began trying his own business ventures almost immediately. While the early ones were failures, he stuck with it (showing discipline) and was able to succeed with a magazine at the age of 18. Over time he built the Virgin empire and acquired his billions.

Anybody who has followed the Virgin brand would know that it has had many business failures as well. Yet the brand is still well liked all over the world and pulling in huge profits. Why? Is it because Branson is an amazing all around businessman? You might think so, but no. Instead, he is a man who **knows his strengths and weaknesses**.

He maximizes his strengths (like his amazing leadership and marketing abilities) and lets other specialists deal with his weaker areas. He also manages to oversee the Virgin empire with the same 24 hour day we all have – yet how many times have you heard people say they "don't have time" for something? Life is all about managing things – managing your strengths and weaknesses, managing your time to be efficient, managing your routine so you are focused on the areas that give the most return.

You can apply this same mindset to willpower and get more out of your day. Remember, making an engine more efficient will help the fuel to last longer. So how do you get more efficient with willpower? The first trick is to use schedules and habits. We covered some of this already. When something becomes a habit through repetition, it becomes more natural to do the habit than to NOT do it. Now you're saving willpower, because the real willpower cost would come from breaking routine and NOT doing the habit. By sticking with it, your willpower stays intact.

Routines are a big help for willpower. Imagine that you have 10 different tasks to do, some more important than others. If you're given a list of these 10 tasks, you still have to figure out the best order to do them in. This costs mental energy and time, draining your willpower too. Now imagine that you're starting the day without any clue of what you need to do – you have to first think of the different tasks, then create an order to do them, then try to remember that order ... and then actually DO THE TASKS! All of this sounds pretty tiring already, right? Especially when you compare it to the ideal alternative – a prepared list of 10 tasks that are already listed in the order you should do them. Doesn't that sound a lot easier?

By having this type of schedule, we remove a lot of the stress and thought process that goes into the daily "planning" stage. It's so much easier to just follow a list without thinking, and it saves your mental energy for the tasks themselves. This is a great way to extend how far your discipline goes.

Using the right order is important too. This comes back to knowing yourself and your strengths/weaknesses. Some people prefer to start easy and slowly build up to the hardest tasks, because momentum is important for them. Others like to start with the hardest, smash it out of the way, then carry on knowing that the day will keep getting easier. Personally, I have a different approach. I like one or two easier tasks to "warm up" and get some momentum going. This makes it easier for me to do the hard tasks afterwards. I still like to get the hardest tasks done in the first half of the day though, because I know I'm most productive in the mornings. After that, the tasks get easier and the day flows nicely.

Scheduling daily tasks is the best way to help your willpower, but you can also create plans and schedules that cover other areas of life. For example, you can base your daily schedule on your to-do list and your overall life plan, ticking off bigger goals as you go along. You can also go more in-depth and create schedules for individual areas of your life, like your work or your diet. The more control you have, the more your discipline will grow.

By using plans, schedules, and habits, you are setting yourself up for success. Living in this type of disciplined environment will see immediate changes.

WILLPOWER RECOVERY

We already touched on a healthy lifestyle for willpower recovery, but we didn't touch a couple of important areas. The areas we covered were relaxation, exercise, and diet. If you want more information on relaxation methods like meditation, I have created some in-depth standalone guides for you. Now we will also go into a bit of detail on sleep.

Sleep is hugely important for maintaining mental discipline. With high levels of discipline, you will be able to work effectively even while tired. First though, you have to build that level of discipline – and that's a lot easier if you're well rested.

Always prioritize sleep. Unless it's an emergency, you're better off being well rested. Being well rested means everything works efficiently and gets done better or faster. This increases your daily output – important if you want to manage your willpower and stay disciplined.

Most people need six to eight hours of sleep a night. You might need a little less or more, but try to always get the right amount. Getting too little (or too much!) can have negative effects.

Outside of night time though, you can also use naps to refresh yourself and restore some willpower. Humans tend to sleep in roughly 90 minute sleep cycles, though this can vary a little. If you've ever woken up very groggy and found it hard to get going for a while, it's likely that you woke up at the wrong part of your sleep cycle – the deep sleep part. Because of these cycles, you should either try to nap for roughly 90 minutes (to get a full cycle), or for 15 to 25 minutes (so you don't slip too deeply into a cycle). If your body is extremely tired, it will often do a "fast cycle," which is like a 90-minute cycle in roughly 15 to 20 minutes. If it isn't that tired, you'll still get a good refresh from the short nap, and you shouldn't be left with any grogginess.

Napping is one way to recharge your meter a little. Another method is taking a break to enjoy a snack or some quick exercise. Be sure to fully break away from your regular grind and enjoy this break for 15 to 20 minutes. You'll feel better and more focused afterwards. Meditation is another method that works to recharge willpower. There are some other methods open to you, including hypnotism and sound therapy.

CHAPTER 12: CREATING A POSITIVE SELF

If you were to come across a guy sitting on a park bench dressed in rags and with an awful smell, would you believe he was a hardworking and productive guy?

Okay, now imagine that you've just woken up, rolled over in your bed, and caught sight of the clock saying 11 a.m. You get up slowly to see your messy room with stuff strewn all over the place. You need a haircut, a shave, and a shower. Your clothes all need washing. Yesterday you didn't even get out of bed, which is why there are dirty plates around the room and stains on the duvet. What's your first step to getting this mess, and yourself, cleaned up? Or do you just put it off until later, or even tomorrow, since it's already almost afternoon anyway?

Having a bad image isn't just about what other people see, it's about what you see and feel. To build and maintain discipline, you have to see yourself as a disciplined person! If you woke up at 5 a.m. purely out of habit, feeling well rested, knowing that your life is well organized and everything you need to do today has been scheduled beforehand – wouldn't that be a much easier way to get going?

To get to that stage takes a little effort though, but remember – it's better to be the one who already climbed the mountain than the one who is still climbing. Get it done once and all you have to do is maintain it.

WHO DO YOU WANT TO BE?

Human life is amazing to me. It finds a way to adapt and survive in almost any circumstance. People can be born with all of the advantages in life – a rich and powerful family, good looks, athletic talent, and a wonderful upbringing around the best type of people. Yet sometimes they will still go way off the rails and throw it all away.

On the flipside, some people are born in terrible circumstances and suffer through horrific childhoods in war-torn countries. They grow up with no family, having been massively traumatized, yet they go on to achieve incredible things.

The point is that your background and current circumstances don't matter. There are rich people who suddenly go broke, and homeless people who suddenly become millionaires. What matters isn't what happens to them or how the world sees them. What matters is **how they see themselves.**

First you have to know what type of life you want and what your goals are. Then you have to figure out **what type of person** lives that life. Really get into it – how does this person think? What does their day-to-day life look like? What type of decisions do they make? What drives them, and how does their mind work? These are all patterns that you need to emulate.

If you can act as that person acts, then you will eventually have what that person has. Think about it, if you can literally match Elon Musk for creativity, work-rate, and business decisions, then you can also literally create the same levels of company he has. By being a similar type of person, it's logical that you'd be able to attract similar friends, business contacts, and romantic partners. I'm not talking about literally becoming Elon Musk; I'm talking about being that level of person.

BUILDING YOUR NEW SELF

Building a new self takes consistent effort, which is good because that also builds your mental discipline. Envision this new you, the disciplined you. Try to spend a little time each day doing this visualization – picture the life you would have and the options that would be available to you. Not only is visualization good for attracting what you want, it's also good for creating a new way of behavior for yourself.

Start by creating a basic checklist of what you need to do to become the person you want to be. Everything should be reflective of this persona. If you are aiming to be a confident person, start acting confidently! That doesn't mean you have to become an extrovert, but it means that you need to take some pride in yourself and your appearance. Speak and think in a way that exudes confidence. Don't speak doubtfully, speak decisively. Your thoughts also shouldn't be about whether you can do something or not, they should be about **finding a way** to do what you have already decided on – after all, you're going to **make it happen**, right?

Your thoughts become your words, which become your actions, which shape you. Body language is another important area. Standing strongly with a straight back and your shoulders up and wide is a strong stance. Don't believe me? Try to stand like that for a couple of minutes and take some deep breaths. I bet you feel more confident.

For the opposite effect, slouch down and make yourself small. Look at the floor, talk quietly and nervously with a lot of hesitation. Quite soon you'll start feeling lower. Stand back up straight, strut around a little, talk loudly and confidently. Hell, shout a bit if you want to! This will instantly release those feel good hormones and have you genuinely feeling more confident. Tricks like these are used by performers all over the world to get into a positive mind state before show time.

Sometimes life will throw bad situations at you to try and break this new you – don't fall for it. Remember how the new you would react and focus on that. You can also use mindfulness breaks to stop emotional reactions and keep yourself on course.

There are a couple of techniques in NLP (Neuro-Linguistic Programming) that can be helpful in dealing with bad events. The first is reframing. Let's say something has just happened that upset or angered you, but it isn't major enough to warrant breaking discipline. It could be a bad day at work, an argument with your spouse, whatever.

What you need to do is imagine the event just as it happened. As you are playing this through your imagination, put a literal frame around the memory – a bright, funny designed one. Back this up by replacing the audio in your memory with ridiculous sounds like circus music or babies laughing. Repeatedly envision the memory, and keep on imagining extremely ridiculous and funny things happening around the memory. This will fry the memory circuits and break the short-term grip that this memory has on your mind. It's a great way to stop something from bothering you.

The second method is dissociation. Here you can either be visualizing a memory of something that's bothering you or an emotion you're struggling with. Visualize that you are now outside of yourself and that you're observing the scene unfold. Zoom out on the scene really far, far enough that you can see the entire block (assuming you're in a building). See how your situation or emotion isn't really affecting anything else?

Zoom out further, far enough to see the whole town, then the country, then right out into space. Is anything being changed or affected by your situation? Now zoom back in, nearly all the way so you can see yourself again. How do you feel about the memory/emotion now? Observe as if you were an onlooker, seeing the original reaction of yourself. This is helpful to analyze how you're behaving in an objective manner. This visualization will leave you in a more rational state of mind when you leave it.

Both of these techniques work well for dealing with setbacks. Use them to maintain your discipline, and keep on being the person you want to be.

STAYING ON COURSE

When you've begun the transformation, you have to maintain it. It's important to be brutally honest with yourself. During a bad run in the 2015-16 season, NBA legend Kobe Bryant described himself as "the 200th best player in the league" and said he "freaking sucks." This wasn't a sentiment on his ability as a player, it was a reflection on his recent performances. Anybody can mess up and get things wrong. What matters is that you put it right.

Always track your performance on this transformation. Note down how disciplined you're actually being. If you're falling off in multiple places because you're pushing too hard, just be honest and dial it back a bit, temporarily. Reward yourself when you are going to plan, but don't do it in a way that contradicts your discipline and the new you.

Consistent effort is the true path to lasting change. Find the areas where you are slacking a little and fix them. See where you can maximize your potential even more and get even more disciplined. Positive affirmations are a helpful way to reinforce the new you, along with visualization.

Maintain your effort by keeping yourself happy and in a positive frame of mind. Take breaks when needed, even if that means a short vacation. The happier you are the more productive and disciplined you will be.

Understand yourself as a person and what drives you. Use this knowledge to incentivize a discipline life.

CHAPTER 13: HACKING YOUR WAY TO BETTER DISCIPLINE

People are always looking for shortcuts in life. It's human nature to want a lot from life, but that takes a lot of effort and a lot of discipline. Businesses thrive on the back of this laziness that affects society. Health, fitness, and beauty are all big industries where shortcuts are heavily advertised. There are companies hawking workout programs, magic pills, and all sorts of other shortcuts to good looks and success. The internet is full of get-rich-quick schemes and scams, too, because this is another area where people want a shortcut.

In reality, we can all figure out the truth. Most people know deep down that there is no shortcut. If there was, everybody would already be taking it, wouldn't they?

Sometimes people can get lucky in life and get a "shortcut" of sorts. This isn't usually a good thing though. Have you ever heard the phrase "it's about the journey, not the destination"? This is a powerful quote that I didn't truly understand the first time I heard it. Now I understand that this phrase is focused on the lessons you need to learn on your journey to success.

A person with low confidence might believe that they need to look physically better in order to feel happier. When they reach that goal, they are likely to actually feel a lot happier. Is it because they have a body that looks different? Only partially – it's also because they've learned how to be confident while working out, and they've gained self-belief that they *can change their lives!*

Another person might be pushing hard in the business world. They achieve success by putting together successful deals and earning money. Now are they in a better position because they have that money or because they have learned the ability to earn that money?

In the above example, I've only listed one main lesson that has helped those people. Every journey has a lot more lessons to learn. For the physical transformation, that person must have learned to handle their diet better. They must have found ways to motivate themselves and to stay disciplined, plus the ability to push hard during exercise. The better these lessons are learned, the better the results will be. The businessman or businesswoman will have learned how to manage money better, how to manage risks, how to spot good deals, and how to set and hit goals. All of this is what makes him or her better with money and able to succeed. Without these lessons, this individual couldn't have his/her current success anyway.

The perfect example of a life shortcut failing is the lottery. Almost everyone believes they would be financially set for life if they were to be handed $1 million or more. This is exactly what happens to lottery winners, but around 70% of them end up broke. **70%!**

It happens because they've never learned to manage their cash properly. They haven't learned how to make money work for them, how to stay disciplined, and how to live within their means. It's just like somebody who goes for liposuction to lose weight, then slowly piles it back on – a shortcut doesn't teach the important lessons needed for actual, lasting change.

With discipline, you have to keep this in mind when you approach it. You have to stay strong willed and focused, even when the inevitable bad times happen. It isn't something that can just be handed to you, because there are lessons to be learned along the way as well. It's normal to fail occasionally and slip off, but the important thing is that you drive onwards in the long term. Aim to improve a little every day, and the goal is inevitable.

While there isn't a shortcut to high discipline, there are a few tips that can help keep you moving in the right direction – or at least block some of the off-ramps into the lands of poor discipline and failure.

TIPS AND TRICKS

Here's a quick hotlist of tips to help you build a disciplined mind and self. Some of these have been mentioned earlier but are still collected here so you can refer to the list with ease.

- Build habits. Habits are one of the easiest ways to stay disciplined. For example, let's say you want to start exercising in the mornings but find it hard to get up and actually pull it off. If you can approach it intensely and force the same wake up time every day for 30 days, then it will feel much more natural to wake up at that same time even on days off. The key is that you **have to enforce it every day** until the habit is built! In the future, if you really need/want a lie in, you can do that – keep it rare and it won't affect your habit. Other habits and routines can be built in the same way – a night routine to help you sleep well, a morning one to start the day fresh and relaxed, eating habits which keep you healthy. All of these can be built with an intense approach for the first month. It's like condensing all the hard parts of discipline into that month so that these habits happen automatically and without difficulty from then on. Habits and routines don't drain any willpower either. Create as many as you can so your willpower is free for other decisions.

- A schedule is another little hack to keeping your willpower high. It lowers the drain on your mental energy because you don't need to make decisions, and more importantly, you don't need to resist temptation. Like habits, this saves your willpower for other things. Schedules are different from habits because a habit is something you would do virtually every day. Using a schedule is how you organize your day around the usual routines and knock out any other goals – like working on your side business or building a network. Listing the tasks removes some thought from your daily planning, plus it stops you from forgetting anything. You can either just list the tasks for the day or put them all in order to remove another drain on your decision-making engine.

- Speaking of temptation, we want to remove as much of it as possible. Temptation is a problem for all of us – when it's late and you're hungry it's pretty tough to avoid that chocolate bar if it's staring you right in the face. People can't binge on junk food if they don't buy it. They can't procrastinate from work on the internet if they've set up a web blocker for recreational sites. These are examples of how you can remove temptation from your life. Your discipline is improved by making better decisions, and better decisions are always going to happen if you can **remove the bad options**. How can you regularly drink too much if you stop keeping alcohol in the house? How can you overspend if you never carry your card? Most of us can make an immediate impact on our discipline by following this tip.

- On the flipside, make the good options more easily available. If part of your plan is to read more instead of watching television, then get the TV out of your bedroom and keep some books near the bed instead. Want to eat healthier? Keep a good stock of pre-prepared healthy snacks. Need to work out more? Get some home equipment so you can do it right there! Human beings like the path of least resistance, so make it as easy as possible to pick the "right" choice. Sticking to a nutritional plan is a lot easier if you use meal prep for example, because the right meal is also the easiest option at this time.

- There's another little trick that I use to help the good decisions too – a rewards system. A reward system gives you something back for staying disciplined and making good decisions. The tricky part is choosing the right rewards and the right frequency. For example, if you reward yourself for eating healthily all day with an unhealthy snack at night, you're going to be eating a lot of bad food by the end of the week. This is also going to mess with healthy eating as a habit or routine, because your system will expect the junk food daily. Instead, you could use a night out as your reward for eating healthy all week, or you could reward yourself with a gift. Either of these wouldn't affect your eating or the building of a new habit/routine. I eat quite well naturally, and exercise a lot too. My problem areas used to be procrastination with work and waking up early. I built those habits by rewarding myself with tasty treats and the occasional day off training (usually to catch a movie or see a friend). This way I was able to build the habits I wanted (and the discipline) while still enjoying life, because the missed workout or odd treat won't affect my highly disciplined approach to health and fitness.

- An accountability partner is a good way to improve your discipline. Most people find it easier to motivate somebody else than to motivate themselves. This is because you see problems from the outside with an objective view. It's kind of like the dissociation NLP technique mentioned in Chapter 12, because you see the facts of the problem without the emotional side attached. You can come up with the right solution and approach pretty easily this way and advise your friend to take that path. One warning – make sure your accountability partner is as serious about this as you so they can actually be depended on to try hard and stay focused. You can help each other during the bad times by offering an outlet to vent to while also giving good advice. Tell each other what your current goals are and how you're progressing as well. Keep a checklist of what your partner is aiming to do, and check in to make sure they're on track. A quick text asking if they worked out today is easy to do. If you're the one being asked and you respect your accountability partner, it's going to prompt you to go get that workout in if you haven't already. This subtle pressure is a great way to keep yourself motivated and on track, because letting yourself down is weirdly easier than letting down other people.

- Being action oriented makes a big impact on your discipline. It's tough to believe but a lot of people mess up *just by overthinking!* They're so caught up in what to do first, or which task is important enough to do now, that they drain their own mental energy *without actually doing anything!* In a few pages, we'll explore what this means a bit further. To sum it up though, it means less thinking and more doing. If you have anything that you know needs to be done, get started on it immediately.

- Don't overload yourself when planning out your schedule or goals. If you have a schedule that is jam packed already, it only takes one thing to go wrong or one delay to make you start feeling the pressure. Be generous with your planning and consider that things can go wrong, and emergencies can pop up too. Keeping your mental state clear and healthy is important to long term success, so help yourself out by keeping a steady, sustainable work rate.

- It's good to aim high with your goals, but it's also important to be realistic. Getting the right balance here should motivate you; it should fire you up and create a drive to reach this goal. The goal has to be tough enough to keep you driven in this way. What you don't want though is a goal that looks doubtful from day one. That drains your energy because it creates a negative state. Stay positive minded and productive by making sure the goal is attainable if you can stay on track around 70-95% of the time. The number you choose should be based on how successful you already are with discipline, and always be aiming for higher numbers each year.

ALL POSITIVITY, NO NEGATIVITY

Look closely at the tips and advice given in this guide so far. You'll see that there's a big focus on the positive side, not much on the negative. I don't like the use of punishments for failing to hit goals, because it can create a bad state of mind. Any negativity that affects your mind or spirit is a bad thing. Reward yourself for doing well, but don't punish yourself if you fail – just don't reward yourself either.

Self-love and a positive self-image are important to creating the foundation of your new, disciplined self. You need to see yourself in a favorable light so you can achieve your goals.

If you could see the selection process for some of the world's special forces units, you might be surprised by how the instructors behave. They don't shout at recruits or belittle them. They don't tell them when they're doing badly or need to pick it up. On the other hand, they also don't praise them or tell them when they're doing well. Throughout the whole thing they stay mostly silent, watching and instructing without giving an opinion or any other feedback. This is hard for a lot of people because they rely on praise or other feedback that they're doing well. That isn't what the special forces need though; they need strong minds that are able to survive without external praise.

Without feedback, most people will start to think negatively. When tiredness, cold, and hunger are having an effect, it's so easy to start losing hope and fall into a spiral of negative thinking and self-doubt. The importance of staying positive can't be overstated. The difference between the soldiers who pass and fail these tests usually comes down to who is the toughest mentally. Those who pass have incredibly resilient minds.

You might not have the toughest mentality today, but you can build up towards achieving it. Remember that everybody has a similar level of potential and focus on keeping your mindset right. Over time, it will become natural to stay positive even in the face of difficulty.

Avoiding punishments, using rewards, and staying positive are all important to **keeping your morale up**.

Another important part of this is **self-care**. Practicing good self-care means looking after yourself properly and keeping yourself happy. A balanced life is the key to this. Don't deprive yourself of social stimulation and enjoyment. Keep this in mind when you're designing the "new you." Your routines and schedules should have some time built into them for leisure; it's as important as exercise, relaxation, and good nutrition. To keep a high level of output you have to maintain the machine that produces it, right? In this case, you are the machine, and the output is your discipline.

Keeping a log of your activities is helpful for analyzing your mental progress with your overall plan. In a similar way, keeping a diary of your feelings can be helpful for the emotional, self-care side. Creating a log has two main benefits, one short-term and one long. The short-term benefit is that you become more aware of your feelings. Just taking a few minutes at the end of each day, you will be more in touch with your feelings. For people who are more emotionally closed, it can take a few weeks of work to even start tapping into what's really below the surface. It's worth the effort, so get started immediately. Being more aware of your feelings allows you to deal with them better, before they become a problem.

In the long term, you can look over a log and start identifying patterns on when you feel down. Keep your schedules and progress lists to check this off against and see what causes you to be down. Are there times with a heavy workload that seem to cause you distress or discomfort? Do you seem to be going in a cycle, with down patches coming at regular intervals? Are the bad feelings happening more when you slack off in a specific area, like exercise or diet? All of this information is important. Approach it without emotional attachment and stick to the facts. An honest overview will give you areas to focus on for change, which will then make you even better and more disciplined.

Another thing to keep in mind with self-care is your **long-term plan**. It's a small minority that wants to just dominate their area day in, day out. Most people are working towards something – their discipline exists to create a desired lifestyle. That lifestyle should always have some discipline involved just for the sake of living a happy, healthy, and productive life. With that said, most of us definitely want to enjoy our time as well.

Think about that when you make your life plans moving forwards as well. If something is going to be part of your long-term plan (e.g. tennis, yoga, or travelling) then you might as well start trying to incorporate it as soon as possible. It will keep you happier and can act as a reward. Good, positive goals like this will also help in other areas of your life that affect discipline, like exercise or happiness. It can even be something as simple as video games. If video games are a big source of happiness for you, then incorporate them into your routine. Remember to limit the time and stick to your planned limits as well, otherwise it goes against discipline. Everybody should be able to enjoy life, but if you want to succeed, then you have to limit the fun for now, so you can live however you want to in the future.

CHAPTER 14: APPLYING YOUR DISCIPLINE

Τhe last chapter covered tips for the planning and preparation areas of mental discipline. This chapter focuses more on putting those plans into action and making the most of your time.

Jocko Willink has a simple motto that sums up the best reason to have discipline.

"Discipline equals freedom."

It's true, and it's the biggest reason for people to pursue discipline so much. Discipline creates results and rewards. Discipline shapes your life into what YOU want it to be. Discipline gives you the money, the connections, and the options to have the **freedom** you desire - so let's get to it!

MACHINE MANAGEMENT AND MOMENTUM

Each day is a new challenge, a clean slate to start from in the morning. Always look at your life in this way. The real reward for a great, productive day is in how it gets you closer to your goals. Your goals are your ultimate reward, so there shouldn't be any need to slack off because you're doing well. In fact, that would be counter-productive.

Of course you'll remember that we talked about balance a bit earlier in the book. Balance is important because a happy, healthy human being is more productive than an unhappy or stressed one. Do what needs to be done so that this balance is always kept. Use the rewards systems to treat yourself and stay happy. The focus should be on your overall happiness and maintaining a good level so that you can be productive and disciplined.

If you are already quite happy and morale is high, then you might as well capitalize by staying active and disciplined. Rewards aren't as important here, because a motivated person already produces well and doesn't need extra incentives. On the flipside, an unhappy person might need more rewards and a less demanding schedule than usual. Think of it as **managing your machine** and deciding what approach will work best. If you're feeling low, it's better to focus on maintaining yourself. When your morale improves and you are able to handle setbacks and pressure a little better, you can start working more on the actual discipline side. It's a smart approach that keeps you from burnout and can also be used to improve your productivity – because most people are starting from a less-than-ideal state of mind.

Another benefit of treating each day as a clean slate is that it helps to make you push harder. Let's look at professional sports for an example of this. In professional sports, there has always been a focus on the form, or recent performances, of different players. Any sportsman or woman can put in an extra good performance once in a while, and they can also put in bad ones. Sometimes there are sportsmen or women who are considered the best in their area, yet they fail to perform for a while. When this happens their "form" is bad, or they're on a bad streak/in a slump. The opposite would be an athlete who's hit a hot streak and is playing above expectations.

The expectation for any athlete is based on how they usually perform – their skill level, morale, fitness, and plenty of other things can play a part. It's not a science, because each person is affected differently by the same situations, depending on factors like past experiences, mental toughness and resilience, self-belief, and more. Some of these areas are important to mental discipline as well, so by having strong discipline, an athlete can be less vulnerable to slumps and improve their chances of hot streaks.

Hot streaks are good for confidence and self-belief, but they can sometimes lead to overconfidence. The problem with a hot streak is that the media and fans get caught up in it – they are living in the past, basking in yesterday's success, and taking it for granted. This is one of the worst things that the athlete themselves could do. If you want to be successful in life, you need the same type of driven mindset that an athlete has. You need to be able to avoid any ego or overconfidence that can come from getting good results. You have to be able to wipe the slate clean at the end of each day, week, or month.

It's important that you acknowledge and appreciate your wins so that you can learn and grow from them. They can fuel you in a positive way and create even more drive. Just make sure you don't rest on your laurels while there's still work to be done – when you're still working towards that final, end goal. For the person who is on form and pushing hard with discipline, having a fresh slate each morning is a challenge. It's a chance to push hard and prove yourself again, making your mark in life and progressing towards your goals. This is the best way to take advantage of the momentum you have going for you; it's easy to be fired up and to *expect* good results on a hot streak. Your efforts have maximum impact, so don't ever slack off during this time. Use your mental discipline to make the most of it, and get as close to your goals as possible.

Hot streaks seem pretty easy to deal with then, but what about slumps? Ups and downs are commonplace everywhere. Sports, businesses, even nations as a whole – everything is always improving or declining, nothing stays constant for long. Whether you call it a slump, a rut, a hole, or anything else, they all mean the same thing – a patch where your performance has declined and isn't up to the usual standard. This "standard" is what you have set for yourself through your goals, through your self-image, and through your actions/performance.

Getting out of a rut can be tough because of the negative momentum you're working against. A rut will sap your motivation and do it's best to wear down your discipline. The positive rewards and feedback are harder to come by, and it's in these depressing situations that you are expected to do even more and work even harder to try and get out of it.

The first thing I want to do is stop that negative frame of mind. Bad times happen, every roller coaster has to have downs to go with the ups, and your journey has to be harder at times and easier at others. There is an ancient proverb that sums these ideas up well. It says:

"This too shall pass."

This applies to good as well as bad and is one of my favorite quotes for helping to keep your ego in check and your mind balanced. To get through a slump, you have to understand that it isn't about you or being undeserving of success – it's about the hard parts of the journey and learning how to navigate them. Remember the lottery winners – your goal is useless if you get there without learning the important lessons that would allow you to repeat the success if needed. Keep calm and breathe. Accept that times are tough. Get hold of your thoughts and emotions with the techniques you've learned and start reshaping them into more constructive beliefs.

In really bad times, you might have to navigate feelings of helplessness or the effects of poor mental health. Depression can be hugely limiting and can even bring people so low that they stop trying, falling into a downward spiral. If any of this begins to happen, you should seek the help of a medical professional as soon as possible.

Make use of the network around you as well; look to your close friends and family for emotional and mental support if you're struggling with something. The belief of being strong and silent is a modern-day illusion. Once more, it goes back to the millennia of evolution that humans have been through.

Over those hundreds of centuries, we have always been social, tribal animals. Even indigenous tribes today, those that have avoided technology and modern development, still live the same type of lifestyle. These people, and all humans of the past, regularly have social time where they discuss their ideas and lives. It's almost like a form of group therapy where people have simple conversations as part of the pack, airing out any problems and getting closure and advice on how they're feeling. This has always been important to having a healthy mental and emotional state, but it has been pushed out of modern society in the past couple of centuries. There are lots of theories on why this happened, some crazier than others, but regardless of the reasons why, we have ended up with a lifestyle that prioritizes being busy and faking happiness above our own health (mental, emotional, and even physical).

Working Through Tasks

Capitalizing or correcting your momentum is all good, but how do you *actually* do those things?

The first technique that will help you get through your schedule is called **chunking**. The first definition of chunking is as a psychological learning technique. It means breaking down a big piece of information into smaller, more manageable chunks. For example, let's say you're studying the second world war. There are lots of different events that are part of the story, from the pre-war times to the post war. Then there's all the battles, knowing who joined in and when, and how everything was unfolding between 1939 through 1945. It's a lot of information to try and remember, especially if you look at it as one big block.

With chunking, you would break it up into smaller pieces. You might focus on learning what happened year by year, or learning what happened based on the countries involved. The approach you take doesn't matter, what's important is that you can break information down into small chunks, each chunk having no more than five to eight pieces of information. The average short-term memory can store around seven pieces of information immediately. After this, they have to be repeated enough to transfer into the long-term memory before any more short-term information can be taken in. If you try taking in more information without properly learning the first seven pieces, they will be lost and forgotten.

In the same way that you can learn easier by tackling manageable chunks, you can also be more productive by using this technique. In this case, chunking is an approach to dealing with your tasks or to-do list. When you look at your goals, they might (and should) seem pretty big and intimidating. We deal with this by breaking each goal down into steps and focusing only on what's in front of you. With chunking, you can use that same process to deal with any task or challenge put in front of you.

Let's say that you need to give your house a deep clean. It's a big job, and it can be hard to start because you know this will have a lot of steps, and it's going to take a while. With chunking, you break the job down into smaller parts, and the size of the chunks is totally down to you. You can only deal with one task at a time anyway, so why would you want the mental pressure and stress of the next five spinning around your head as well? It's much better to pick one job/chunk and get started.

For the house cleaning, let's pretend that your starting chunk is "cleaning the bedroom." Now that doesn't sound too bad, right? If it does, break it down again. Start by making your bed, or even just opening the curtains. The important thing is that you get started, because even a tiny step creates a little bit of positive momentum. If you look around and try to do every little task (five minutes or less) that you can find, then you're going to notice tasks getting knocked off pretty quickly anyway. The momentum will make you feel better, too, so it's easier to move on to the next chunk.

These little chunks eventually take care of your bedroom, so then you take another room and break that one down as well until it's done. You end up sorting the entire house room by room, all without the pressure of completing the task playing any part.

Time, Intensity, and Action

Speaking of **five minutes or less**, this is another cool trick that helps you stay disciplined and productive. Planners and schedules are great tools for helping to shape the life you want, but if you overuse them, they can be counter-productive. Nobody should need to put "take out the trash" or "brush your teeth" on the list. These are all normal tasks; get them done as soon as they need doing. Absolutely *anything* which only takes around five minutes or less should be done immediately. These are the little jobs that can affect your mental and emotional state if you let them pile up. Get them knocked out immediately instead, and you'll feel less stressed, plus it builds the habits of immediate action and discipline, creating the self-image of a doer.

Speaking of **immediate action**, that's the name of our next tip. Breaking down the big jobs into chunks is a great trick for boosting or maintaining your mental state because the job doesn't seem as long or difficult. It's easier to get started by using this approach, and **getting started is the most important step**.

Back when I was studying at university, I would sometimes struggle with the big assignments. Having to come up with a 10- or 20-*thousand* word essay? I've never met anybody who looked forward to this kind of task. Even breaking it down into chunks can still be a bit intimidating, because whether it's five thousand or one thousand words, it still feels like a lot. Plus in this type of situation, chunking is a little less helpful. If each chunk is basically doing the same thing again, then it still seems like a tough task to start. Writing 1,000 words can feel tough. Imagine writing them while *knowing* that you'll have to repeat the process 10 or 20 more times.

Here's where **immediate action** has its best impact. With immediate action, you don't even worry about the chunks or the end. You literally just focus on making a start. Got 20,000 words to do? Great, just make a start; see if you can write 100. By the time you get started and do 100 words, you probably need to do more just to finish your paragraph or the point you're explaining. This can easily take you to a few hundred words, or even a thousand. Eventually this first burst will start to fade away, and your point will be made. Know what to do now? Start on the second point. Just start, that's all. Sometimes you will start and fade away before too long, leaving a point half made – but hey, at least you've got maybe a couple thousand words more than nothing, right? Next time you might even maintain the momentum and keep going for longer than expected.

At university, there were times when I struggled and had to "just start" every day, grinding an assignment down with a thousand words or so each time. Other times I would get into a flow after starting, and the words would just pour out of my fingertips and on to the screen. On these days, I could get more than half of my assignment done at once – there were even times when I finished the whole thing in one sitting!

Getting started is another trick that works with the idea of momentum. By making a start, you have done the part that takes the most effort – going from standing still to moving forwards. Now it can be easier to keep going than it is to stop, at least for the early stages. You'd be surprised how much can be accomplished with this technique. Give it a try and see for yourself!

THE FIRST STEP

Most people struggle with this first step because they put so much importance on it. There are people out there who put way too much time and effort into creating a plan or deciding what order to tackle the tasks in. There are also people who don't start because they are worried they won't produce their best work. In either case, the worst thing that you can do is to not start. To quote Mike Tyson:

"Everybody has a plan until they get punched in the face."

Iron Mike is a legend, and this quote is referring to how people would try and create a strategy for dealing with him. Creating a strategy is great, it's a good idea, and it can really help your chances in life. The problem comes when you're creating a strategy from the outside, without experiencing the situation. People who fought Mike Tyson were making strategies based on *fighting other people*! They had never been in the ring with Mike before, so how would they know if it was really going to work or not? They didn't!

Focus on getting stuck in to the situation, getting started, and doing what you can. Yes, it's good to have a plan, but that plan might have to change rapidly once you actually go into action. Be ready for this and be adaptable. As human beings, our biggest strength is that we can adapt to any situation better than other animals. This is why we're the apex species on Earth, and this is the skill you need to focus on if you want to succeed.

Knowing that your plan might not survive first contact is important, and once you accept this, it becomes a lot less important to create the perfect plan or strategy before starting. Remember that one step forward, even a sloppy and unplanned step, is better than the most perfectly planned step that *hasn't* happened yet.

We also have something called the **40% rule**. When I first came across this, it was through ex-SEAL and all-around tough guy, David Goggins. His saying is this:

"When your body and mind are telling you that you're done, you're probably only really around 40% done. That's where most people quit."

At first this was shocking to me, but I heard it around the same time as when I got serious about my physical training. It was suddenly a lot more important to me, and I *knew* I could get the results if so many other people were. This was when I hired a trainer, a guy who had experience with dozens of top athletes.

This guy would leave me feeling fried every day. I was exhausted during some sessions, looking at my trainer and pleading for sympathy, telling him I couldn't do any more. His response? "I know. Now do this." It was unreal! This guy was telling me that he knows I can't do anymore, and that's okay. But do a little more! It felt absolutely maddening, but every time he asked for more, I would try. I honestly expected to fall flat on my face with each push up, or slip off the bar if I tried even one more pull up. But sure enough, one rep at a time, more would come out of me. There were days when I thought I couldn't finish the second set, only to end up pushing all the way through all five. This was amazing, and it proved what Goggins said – most people really do cap out at 40%.

These days I know that when I'm starting to feel tired or drained that there's still a lot more left in the tank. It motivates me and fuels my belief so that I can keep on pushing that little bit further, and that little bit is usually enough to reach my goals.

On the flipside, 40% of your effort and focus is probably enough to move forwards too. Again, it comes back to waiting for the perfect time or perfect plan. Those things just don't happen, and you don't need to be 100% on form to make progress either. If you can give something 40% effort, it's usually enough to move forwards.

Of course it's good to have high standards and always try to produce great work. Realistically though, your best work probably won't be needed very often. When it is, try your best and focus on producing at 100%. This is for those key make-or-break moments. The rest of the time you can get by with less than 100%, and 40% seems to be the golden ratio where your work will be acceptable, progress will be steady, and the pressure isn't too hard either.

Keeping It Interesting

Variation is another thing you should take advantage of. By living a disciplined life, you will sometimes have to deal with difficult or boring tasks. If everything was fun and interesting, there'd be no need for discipline in the first place. As Jim Rohn says:

"Discipline is the bridge between goals and accomplishments."

If you want your goals to become actual accomplishments, you have to stay disciplined to get there. The trick of variation is one that helps you to keep on going through the tough patches, keep on pushing until your task is done.

Let's say you have eight hours of work to do, work that is going to be similar the whole way through. Some people might look at this and want to tackle it head on, smashing all eight hours at once. Firstly, this is a *bad strategy*; it isn't a smart way to tackle this task at all. The head-on approach is a very blunt, brute force strategy for this job. It could work, but it's going to be hard to maintain for most people.

The smarter way to deal with it is to add some **variation** into your day. Break up your eight hours of work into eight, one-hour blocks. In between each block, take a short break to do something different. One of those breaks could be a proper lunch break. Another could be a quick meditation break. Yet another could be time for a quick walk or a little exercise. There are all kinds of breaks you can fit in – exercise, relaxation, food, a bit of socialising, or downtime. Do whatever it takes to keep your productivity high. A break doesn't even have to be all that long, it can just be a few minutes to walk around the room and take your mind off things. Studies have shown that the average human being can concentrate for around 45 minutes at a high level before decline sets in. This time can vary a little from person to person, and it's worth remembering that you don't need 100% attention to be productive (like with the 40% rule).

Experiment with your break times and see what works best. Personally, I take a short break every hour for the first few hours, usually around five minutes. This is enough to get me through the first few hours, after that I'll need a longer one, maybe for some exercise or some lunch. Then the next couple of breaks are short again, followed by longer ones as the end of the day gets closer. Experiment and see what works best for you. Keeping a log of your performance with different break strategies is a good idea as well, because you can see how productive you were with each set up, instead of guessing or basing it on how you feel.

The other way you can use variation is by switching between tasks. Your daily schedule might have a few different types of jobs on there. You might need to do a chunk of work, a chunk of cleaning, and a chunk of admin stuff. You can follow a schedule that rotates a bit of time between each task so you're not stuck at any one thing for longer than a couple of hours. This keeps your mind fresh and your motivation high. It's a lot easier to work for a few hours switching between different tasks than it is to spend many hours on one task at a time. Our brains are built for variation; they enjoy different stimulus and being able to avoid the boredom of being stuck on the same task.

ADAPTATION

We touched on adaptation a few pages back with the Mike Tyson quote of *"Everybody has a plan..."* Being prepared to change your plans is good to start with. This isn't because the plan isn't good – it's because situations are always changing, and you never have the complete picture during the planning stages. The complete picture only comes when you are on the ground and taking action. This is when you find out what problems need to be dealt with.

When you are in motion, any setbacks are signs to modify the *plan* not the *goal*. Keep that strong self-image of yourself and remember your goal to be disciplined. Sports teams will adjust tactics on the move, so do military units. You have to be ready to do the same.

A problem can be dealt with using the same techniques as anything else. Break it down into pieces and see what you need to solve first. Focus on this first job, and find the solution, even if that means trying a few different solutions until you get the right one.

Then you can move to the second issue and more until they've all been solved. If you use this mentality, you can learn how to do *anything*.

Experience will help you to do all of this even better in the future, and it also helps with your discipline, because the more problems you have to deal with, the less they can affect you in the future. Another David Goggins quote:

> *"You have to build calluses on your brain just like how you build calluses on your hands."*

He's talking about enduring tough situations. Goggins does ultra-marathons and a whole variety of other crazily difficult things just to build a strong mind, which has faced difficulty many times. He does the things he hates, in the worst conditions, so he will be mentally strong and disciplined in any situation. Experience with discipline will give you the same benefits. It will strengthen your mind and get you used to being disciplined, which makes it easier to stay disciplined in the future. It even lets you build on your discipline and raise it to higher levels. Remember that you don't want to overwhelm yourself in the early days – it's a marathon, not a sprint. It's better to have continuous, consistent progress that will raise your mental discipline gradually to the highest levels.

CHAPTER 15: BOOSTING YOUR EFFORTS

With the advice given in this guide, you should already be able to greatly improve on your mental discipline. You now have the tools and techniques to create a more disciplined life. We just finished talking about how you can (and should) build on an already disciplined life to make it even better. Everything in life has different levels to it, and by reaching the highest levels of discipline, you will unlock whatever type of life you want.

In sports, it's easy to see the different levels. You have different tiers and levels of sports teams. There are people who perform well at high school level but struggle at anything higher. There are also people who make it all the way to the professional level and are considered star talents. Regardless of the level, there's always room for improvement. One of the best soccer players in the world is Cristiano Ronaldo. This guy has been thought of as one of the best players since he was a teenager and is still performing at the very highest level, aged 34. He's already in the discussion for greatest of all time, yet he is known for a ridiculously high work-rate and a professional, disciplined approach to every area of his life, from diet to recovery. Here are a couple of quotes from him:

"I think I have improved from last year. I am always trying to improve my game and improve myself."

"I still learn."

"I know that no one's harder on me than myself, and that's never going to change."

This is clearly a very driven man. Despite being considered the best player (alongside Messi) in the world for over a decade, he isn't slowing down. In fact, he's still pushing hard to try and get even better. As he's gotten older, his character has matured, and he's been able to become even more professional, even more disciplined.

It's a mentality that everybody should be trying to copy. Constant improvement is the way forward.

Remember this when you are pushing towards your own goals and using the techniques I've taught you. With a good core level of discipline and a good understanding of those techniques, it's possible to develop even further.

TRUE CONTROL

The mind can go off on a tangent and spin towards negative thoughts at any time. It can also throw up intrusive, unhelpful thoughts. Your emotions also have their own reactions to different situations and can mess with you if you fall into a negative state in response to an event in your life. The difference now is that you know how to best deal with this. Sometimes it's still going to be difficult, especially the emotional side. There are some really bad things that can happen in life and they can really throw you out of sync. If you do suffer from a really bad or traumatic event, take your time to heal and process the situation. Maintain what discipline you can, but be gentle and generous with yourself during the process. Once you're ready to go again, you'll be able to build the discipline back up more quickly than before.

With the mental and emotional management techniques in this guide, you can get a great level of control over your own thoughts and emotions. Once you do that, it's possible to move to the next step – understanding other people's thoughts and emotions.

Understanding your own mind, emotions, and psychology are all helpful to understanding general human emotions and thoughts. You will begin to spot people's mindsets. If somebody lacks a lot of self-belief, or has an unfocused mind, you may be able to spot it when interacting with them. This is a helpful tool, because it allows you to guide them through their thoughts/emotions and to better deal with them. You won't be able to control their mental/emotional states, but you will be able to influence them and hopefully bring some discipline to their lives too.

Why does the discipline of other people matter? Because we are all affected by our surroundings. If you're surrounded by undisciplined, negative people, then it will make it a lot tougher for you to stay disciplined, happy, and productive. On the flipside, having positive and disciplined people around will push you to maintain your standard AND try even harder.

Having a positive effect on people is noticeable for them too. It will create a *public image* of you as a disciplined person, which is the next step after your disciplined *self-image*. If viewing yourself as a disciplined person helps to enforce it, adding on the social pressure of *others* viewing you in that way will help as well.

The understanding of emotions and thoughts will become deeper within yourself too. You'll know immediately when something isn't right and will be able to spot signs earlier. This helps you deal with the problem faster and more effectively. Over time, staying in a positive and disciplined state becomes habit, so the work is more about staying on track instead of getting on track.

Maximizing Your Routines

Once more, it's time for you to do some analysis and see how you're progressing. Keeping logs and diaries is very helpful, although it's probably easier to see where you need to make tweaks, thanks to your already high level of discipline. Look for any gaps or areas where you can squeeze out even a small improvement.

It's extremely helpful if you can create some **positive feedback loops** as well, which fuel your desired life goals. For example, if you want to travel and get healthy, but also want to be disciplined with work, then you could reward your work related discipline with interesting fitness or travel related rewards. You might reward yourself by taking up a new hobby sport for example. Taking part in this sport is a reward but also requires discipline, plus it makes you happier and feel rewarded, so you really *want* to push through with work discipline again.

Having the reward will also have refreshed you ready for work. The idea is that when you get back to work (from your holiday or after your exercise session), you will be working even harder and sticking to discipline even more because the reward is fresh in your mind and giving you extra fuel. This gets you more rewards, which makes you work even harder, and so on in a circle until you reach the highest levels possible. This is how you take advantage of positive feedback loops.

Don't forget the **effects of momentum** too. Striking while the iron is hot is how you maximize your development. Once you are moving forward and your discipline is improving, you should never slack off. It takes more energy to start a ball rolling from a standstill than it does to speed it up if it's already rolling. Momentum with discipline works in the same way. If you're already disciplined and moving along that route, then adding a few more tweaks to be even more disciplined isn't too hard. For people who aren't showing any discipline at all, even a couple of simple steps can seem really hard.

Make sure your work isn't wasted by focusing on total development of discipline. Slacking off should never be a reward, being undisciplined should never be a reward, and your belief should be to maintain a disciplined life from here on out. Negative momentum is also real, so if you start to slide, your focus has got to be on stopping it. Stop any deterioration, and then focus on rebuilding discipline afterwards. Deterioration is a big sign of poor discipline; if it happens to you it needs to be nipped in the bud.

An important note – a sudden lowering of discipline can be a sign of unacknowledged mental or emotional issues. Make sure you're truly doing everything possible to deal with these areas and to keep your body, mind, and soul healthy. All three of these areas are interlinked, and you have to develop in each one to live happily (and to be productive while maintaining discipline).

Your **good habits and routines** need to become a permanent part of your life as well. A good way to do this is by anchoring them to essential parts of your day. Got a nice routine going in the mornings? Make brushing your teeth and eating breakfast a final part of that routine, and perhaps even anchor it to a starting signal. The simplest things work best – if opening your curtains each morning is the trigger to begin your routine, then it's easily going to be ingrained in you after a couple of months. It makes the morning routine almost automatic and super easy to get into.

While some habits are tougher than others to anchor, it's possible to do this with all of them. You just have to be a little creative with your triggers and prompts, making sure they work in harmony with your daily life.

CHAPTER 16: DEFENDING YOUR DISCIPLINE

I'd like to share another quote with you. This one has been attributed to a few different people, but I first heard it in an interview with a young, successful entrepreneur. He was talking about his work rate and the consistency of his output, and why it had stayed so high despite his repeated successes in the years before the interview.

"The greatest threat to your future success is your current success."

It's so incredibly true that most people overlook it. It comes back to the difference between drive and motivation. Motivation is fleeting, it's temporary. People feel motivated *sometimes,* then they lose the feeling and fall off the path. Being driven is a different matter. Like Eric Thomas says:

"When you want it as badly as you want to breathe, THEN you will be successful."

To be driven is to be obsessed. It's to be like Cristiano Ronaldo pushing on even though he's considered the best already. It's to be like Tom Brady, a sixth round pick in the NFL draft all those years ago. This man was overlooked by everybody, even his own team, before getting a shot. He was doubted from day one and that created a drive that propelled him to the top spot in his sport. Tom Brady won his first Super Bowl in 2001 during his third season in the sport. A lot of people would be tempted to slack off after hitting this peak. Tom wasn't. They won it again in 2003 and 2004 and had a perfect season in 2007, winning every game until the final.

By that game, Brady was considered one of the greats. He had the fame, the money, the endorsement contracts, AND the supermodel girlfriend. This is where success would start to break most people's discipline. It takes an iron resolve, a real drive, to stay disciplined in the face of all this comfort and all these options. Since then, the Patriots have won another three Super Bowls with Brady leading the team. His success definitely didn't derail him and even in his 40's, he's at the top of his game.

Always remember why you started this journey. Don't allow comfort to weaken your discipline. Until your goals are fulfilled and your plan is completed, there should only be a forward march on discipline.

"No slack whatsoever." – Jocko Willink

CHARTING YOUR PROGRESS

As you walk the self-developmental path, those lists of goals and multi-step plans are important for charting your progress. Working through a plan step by step means you can always see exactly where you're at. It's a good idea to keep a separate checklist that lists the steps of ALL your plans, no matter which area of life it's about. This is like a master list for you to refer to.

When you complete a step, check it off. The aim is to gradually clear the entire list, but clearing it completely would mean that you're stagnating and not pushing as hard as you can – not being as disciplined as you should.

When your list begins to near completion in even one area, it's time to update the list. You have to be setting and updating goals regularly to grow as a person. Even if you're striving to be number one in your field and are coming close, there's always more to do. Even for the greatest there has ever been, there is still room for improvement. The point is to be **the best you can be**, not the best compared to everyone else. The greatest of all time is a mantle that can be passed on in the future, so if somebody were to earn it, they should make the gap as big as possible and try to hold on to it. Knowing you've been the best **you can be** is what discipline is about. People who fail but know they gave their all are able to rest much easier than those who succeeded but believe they could have done better.

Even in the early days when you're creating your plans and goals, you should be ambitious. It's good to have a bigger overall goal in place, then work back from that. If the big goal looks in sight, immediately start thinking about bigger and better ones. Aiming for something that is too close will dull enthusiasm and dampen your drive. Big goals give big inspiration, and they give you the best reason to stay disciplined and productive.

Internal Focus Versus External Focus

The people we talked about, like Tom Brady and Cristiano Ronaldo, are prime examples of people with an internal focus. Bill Gates and Elon Musk are also internally focused; you have to be if you want to keep pushing once you're already reached the top of your field.

Having an internal focus means that you believe you have the ability to shape and influence your life. It's a belief that you have control over your journey, compared to an external focus where people feel that the events and circumstances around them decide their fate. Externally focused people feel powerless and are the types who are relying on luck or waiting for a big break or different circumstances. To succeed, you have to take control of your life and be internally focused.

True internal focus also means that you are focused on internal results. This means that material results don't matter so much; it means that the money you make or the accolades you earn are not the measure of your success. With internal focus, you are **concentrating on maximizing your performance**, your own output. If you've already hit your financial goals but you know that there is room for more discipline and more productivity, then you should still be driving ahead at full speed.

In reality, nobody can ever truly max out, because as you get better, you will also find new ways to improve and new little tweaks to improve your output. Discipline is massive to managing this process; you have to stay disciplined and keep a strong internal focus.

Everybody has a reason to be driven and seek discipline – those who don't have a reason don't begin the search, so by being here, you must have a reason. Always keep this in mind, no matter how long it has been or how much of the journey has been completed. Any pain or struggle from your past that fuels you should always be kept in mind. Relate back to it if you do start feeling too comfortable and remember why you started. For some people, it isn't even a real event that happened, just a determination to avoid bad circumstances – or a determination to succeed and provide a high standard of life for themselves or their families. The reasons can be happy ones as well; you can be fuelled by love and devotion just as easily as pain and struggle. Your specific reasons aren't the important detail here. The important point is to use your fuel constantly to keep your discipline high.

KEEPING YOUR VISION FOCUSED

Your reasons aren't the only thing you should keep in mind. Remember your goals too. Every time they get closer, you need to aim bigger and higher. Of course you don't always need to be 100% focused on a career or financial goals – discipline isn't only about material success. Discipline means making the most out of your life in all areas. If you are reaching your financial or business goals and don't really need much more, you can still use that discipline to better your life in other areas.

By being disciplined, you make the most of your time. That means you could manage the financial needs of your family with comfort by reaching a certain level of success and begin devoting time to your family instead. You can devote more time to your own health and welfare, to relaxation and enjoying life in whatever way you like. Hobbies, social events, and more can be enjoyed. Discipline isn't all about work – it's about learning how to work HARD so you can do more of what you WANT to do. It's about enjoying the life you want to live.

Even the guy who is living a life of hobbies, family, and minimal work should still be striving for more though. He or she could strive to develop more in personal hobbies, or to develop a better relationship with family members. You could spend time with your children and mentor them more, become involved in their lives, and play a more active role in their upbringing. You might want to be more active in the community instead. The field doesn't matter, the point is that there's always a bigger goal. Always aim for bigger goals to keep yourself hungry.

Use **visualization** to keep your goals and your fuel effective. Feel the associated emotions that help you to stay mentally strong and disciplined. Think about your reasons why and the goals you're aiming for.

"I would visualize things coming to me. It would just make me feel better. Visualization works if you work hard. That's the thing. You can't just visualize and go eat a sandwich." – Jim Carrey

It's good to visualize and picture your goals, but be wary that you aren't just hoping to attract it by imagining it. Belief in yourself and a success mindset are important – you have to feel that you ARE disciplined and that you ARE successful to get there. It doesn't happen because you're *visualizing* it though. It happens because you *believe* that you *are* these things, so you *live* in a way that reflects that – including the work, the decisions, and the sacrifices that come along with being that person.

Along with the visualization, you should build habits that reinforce your drive. Make a habit of **analyzing your recent progress** and doing an audit of your results. Be honest with yourself to get the best out of this. Use the **regular positive rewards** to keep fueling your dreams. Visualize some small goals as well so that when you check them off, you've genuinely brought visualized goals into reality. It's all about enforcing the new you – the successful and disciplined you.

Use habits that have visible progress, such as working on fitness. Visual results like this are powerful because they are constant reminders of the work you have already done to build yourself into something more.

DEALING WITH SETBACKS

The final problem you will need to defend your discipline against is the inevitable setbacks. Setbacks will hit you from one place or another eventually – it happens to everyone. It can be something in your personal life or your professional life. It could be a random occurrence that only affects you, or a big disaster that affects an entire industry, area, or family. Disasters come in many forms. They're also a massive test for your mental discipline.

Remember when we talked about self-care? It's important to keep that in mind. You are the machine and it's important that you're healthy and happy. If something bad happens, you must take whatever time is needed to process it. Some situations definitely allow for time away, such as the death of a loved one. What you can't do is let it derail you completely.

Mental toughness and discipline are important if you want to avoid pain and reach your goals. Even if you're only doing a little bit, it all helps. Keep your output to at least 20%, and you will get the most important things done. When bad times hit, process them in a way that works for you. Use methods like meditation if you need to. Big events are difficult to prepare for because there's so much variation in what can happen. Having stayed even a little on course will make a big difference once it's over though.

Smaller things will happen as well, and those are easier to deal with. There are some great techniques that can help you with the more common problems. The solutions we are going to use include **reframing**, **dissociation**, **breathing techniques**, **visualization**, **mindfulness**, and **meditation**.

We looked at **reframing** earlier in the guide, but let's recap it now. When you get certain feelings or thoughts, they aren't really caused by the problem in front of you, instead they're caused by *how you view* that problem. This is why other people might see something as less of a problem (or more) than you do, because we all have our own unique viewpoints. These viewpoints are based on past experience and the lessons we've learned throughout our lives.

When you use reframing, you are altering the way you view a problem by getting rid of the old outlook. You need to get really vivid in your imagination to experience the situation and the negative feelings/thoughts that you associate with it. Give it complete, 100% focus to make it as real as possible to your brain. Then you "frame" the memory with something ridiculous happening, or something funny. It doesn't matter what you imagine (in fact the crazier it is, the better), it just matters that it's outrageous, unrealistic, and not at all scary or intimidating.

Repeat this over and over again with different things happening, and do it rapidly for five minutes or more at a time, reinforcing it a few times each day when starting. This will make you a lot less sensitive to the problems. By overwhelming your memory circuitry with these whacky situations, they lose grip on the negative outlook they used to have and become confused between the fake and silly imaginary scenarios, and the real thing. Now you have a blank slate and a blank state, so you can look at each situation or problem with an objective view and deal with it using an objective, fact-based approach.

Dissociation was also mentioned earlier in the guide. This is when you look at your situation but as an observer instead of from your point of view. It takes a little practice and good visualization or imagination to work. With practice, this can be an extremely powerful technique. It lets you alter your behavior, because when you look at your problems as an observer, you look only at the facts and not the attached feelings or any baggage that you personally have regarding the situation.

Seeing a problem in this way makes solutions clear. You could view it as if some friend or family member had the problem and you're advising them. You can also zoom out and see the problem and your situation as only one small part of the massive world around us all. Unless your problem is a large meteor headed straight for us, or an impending nuclear launch, it's unlikely to be any more than a ripple in the ocean that is Earth. Seeing that your problem isn't so bad makes it more manageable, while looking in from the outside removes your emotional reactions and responses, neither of which have any place in a disciplined approach.

Speaking of **visualization**, it's an effective technique for problem solving as well. Again there's a focus on our outlook and reaction here. You don't have to have an exact solution, you just need to visualize that you CAN and WILL solve the problem in front of you. Problem solving should be part of your self-image, too, because it helps the visualization to become more powerful.

Regularly practice visualizing problems and working your way through them. Visualize how you will stop at nothing and keep a disciplined, high output to get through life. See yourself achieving your goals and succeeding. By visualizing all of this vividly, you will build your own confidence and belief in your problem solving ability. You can also couple all of this with **positive affirmations** to make them even more powerful.

I find that listening to positivity podcasts and videos helps a lot with the affirmation side. It's a little bit like being surrounded by positive people all day – for me, it's the next best thing to having Tony Robbins, Jocko Willink, or Gary Vaynerchuck as my own personal friends and mentors. I use videos daily as a way of surrounding myself with positive affirmations and belief. It helps to keep my discipline at an extremely high level, and I don't even need to take time out of my day for it. I listen to my affirmations and podcasts in the car, while doing chores, and even in the shower/bath.

I have in-depth guides for **mindfulness and meditation** available to you already. Those guides are much more informative and comprehensive than anything I could list here, so if you want to know more, check those out.

Outro

It's been quite a journey through this book so far and if you're still here, then congratulations on sticking with it. You have walked a few more steps along the long path of discipline. In that time, we've explored the makings of discipline, how it works, and how you can adapt it.

Those lessons start in changing your core and your self-beliefs, just as I did many years ago. Creating a new identity in your mind of the person you want to be and enforcing it through small decisions. For me, it started with morning routines during university and moved on from there. I learned to chunk assignments, to grind out hard days with a lower output (but never zero) if needed, and to create plans for my days.

Since then, I've began to strategize my life, control thoughts and emotions, and to aid my development by living a healthier lifestyle – one that includes good diet, exercise, relaxation, and socializing. Pushing outside of the comfort zone in different areas of life has helped as well – and you can benefit a lot from pushing your boundaries in general too.

Remember that life can be what you want it to, if you are really willing to live the lifestyle that goes with it. I mean the *real* lifestyle, not the Hollywood make-believe where rich people get to lie around all day and boss people around. As Jordan Peterson says, the top of the pile is a tough spot to be – everyone looks to you for the answer and solution.

For most of us, we want a moderate amount of success, enough to enjoy life. It's about the lifestyle that will make you happy, and most people don't actually want to be Elon Musk and still working those kinds of hours. Most people want to enjoy the perks way before that time, and that's perfectly okay – I know I'd be happy some distance before the billion dollar mark.

Once you have decided what you really, *really* want (and are willing to put the work in for), then you adapt that persona. Believe in your ability to get there, and back it up with effort. Hold yourself to those new standards and create that identity, ingrain it into yourself, piece by piece.

Live a *healthy life* and take advantage of the energy and productivity boosts from good sleep, diet, and exercise. Use relaxation and socialization to keep yourself in good mental shape too. Build your mental toughness and willpower as you go, one step at a time. Remember this isn't a sprint, it's a long-distance race. To be in it for the long haul, you need to gradually adapt so that you don't overwhelm yourself.

Exercise self-control and begin cutting out your old, bad habits. Again, take it slowly if you need to. Don't overwhelm yourself. Your body and mind are essential parts of the machine that is you, and you need it to work optimally to have the best shot at success. Always take good care of yourself. You wouldn't build a house on a rocky foundation, would you? It's the same premise.

As you develop, a new you begins to take shape. From there, it's time to really get to grips with the planning. Be the mastermind architect of your future, and enforce new habits, adding more as you go. Create those routines and eliminate any remaining bad habits and weaknesses. Begin to really master your thoughts and emotions. This is the area most affected by good relaxation and mental health, so exercise and socialization play a part too – as does diet. It's surprising how much a bad diet can negatively affect your hormone production and mental health, so be sure to stay on point with your nutrition.

Over time, you can keep on increasing your willpower and how effectively you use it by using the techniques learned from this guide. Your improvement will only accelerate, and it's surprising how much can be achieved in even a few years using this approach.

Make sure you give the new you a reason to stick around and make it permanent too. Use those rewards and good times. Enjoy your life, and get out there in whatever way you want sometimes – whether it's doing the nightclub thing or travelling to a remote destination. Life is here to be enjoyed, and if you're happy and enjoying some rewards along the way, it'll only make you happier and work even harder.

Good luck on your journey out there. Many before you have benefitted from the methods within this guide. Now the knowledge is in your hands, and it's up to you whether you want to join them. All the best!

<u>One last thing before you go – Can I ask you a favor? I need your help!</u> If you like this book, could you please share your experience on Amazon and write an honest review? It will be just one minute for you (I will be happy even with one sentence!), but a GREAT help for me and definitely good Karma ☺**.** Since I'm not a well-established author and I don't have powerful people and big publishing companies supporting me, <u>I read every single review and jump around with joy like a little kid every time my readers comment on my books and give me their honest feedback!</u> If I was able to inspire you in any way, please let me know! It will also help me get my books in front of more people looking for new ideas and useful knowledge.

If you did not enjoy the book or had a problem with it, please don't hesitate to contact me at contact@mindfulnessforsuccess.com **and tell me how I can improve it to provide more value and more knowledge to my readers.** I'm constantly working on my books to make them better and more helpful.

Thank you and good luck! I believe in you and I wish you all the best on your new journey!

Your friend,

Ian

Don't hesitate to visit:

-My Blog: www.mindfulnessforsuccess.com

-My Facebook fanpage: https://www.facebook.com/mindfulnessforsuccess

-My Instagram profile: https://instagram.com/mindfulnessforsuccess

-My Amazon profile: amazon.com/author/iantuhovsky

Also, if you haven't downloaded your free book already:

Discover How to Get Rid of Stress & Anxiety and Reach Inner Peace in 20 Days or Less!

To help speed up your personal transformation, I have prepared a special gift for you!

Download my full, 120 page e-book "Mindfulness Based Stress and Anxiety Management Tools" for free <u>by clicking here.</u>

Link:

<u>tinyurl.com/mindfulnessgift</u>

<u>Hey there like-minded friends, let's get connected!</u>

Don't hesitate to visit:

-My Blog: <u>www.mindfulnessforsuccess.com</u>

-My Facebook fanpage: <u>https://www.facebook.com/mindfulnessforsuccess</u>

-My Instagram profile: https://instagram.com/mindfulnessforsuccess

-My Amazon profile: <u>amazon.com/author/iantuhovsky</u>

Recommended Reading for You

If you are interested in Self-Development, Psychology, Emotional Intelligence, Social Dynamics, Soft Skills, Spirituality and related topics, you might be interested in previewing or downloading my other books:

Self-Discipline: Mental Toughness Mindset: Increase Your Grit and Focus to Become a Highly Productive (and Peaceful!) Person

This Mindset and Exercises Will Help You Build Everlasting Self-Discipline and Unbeatable Willpower

Imagine that you have this rare kind of power that enables you to maintain iron resolve, crystal clarity, and everyday focus to gradually realize all of your dreams by consistently ticking one goal after another off your to-do list.

Way too often, people and their minds don't really play in one team.

Wouldn't that be profoundly life-changing to utilize that power to make the best partners with your brain?

This rare kind of power is a mindset. The way you think, the way you perceive and handle both the world around you and your inner reality, will ultimately determine the quality of your life.

A single shift in your perception can trigger meaningful results.

Life can be tough. Whenever we turn, there are obstacles blocking our way. Some are caused by our environment, and some by ourselves. Yet, we all know people who are able to overcome them consistently, and, simply speaking, become successful. And stay there!

What really elevates a regular Joe or Jane to superhero status is the laser-sharp focus, perseverance, and the ability to keep on going when everyone else would have quit. I have, for a long time, studied the lives of the most disciplined people on this planet. In this book, you are going to learn their secrets.

No matter if your goals are financial, sport, relationship, or habit-changing oriented, this book covers it all.

Today, I want to share with you the science-based insights and field-tested methods that have helped me, my friends, and my clients change their lives and become real-life go-getters.

Here are some of the things you will learn from this book:

• **What the "positive thinking trap" means,** and how exactly should you use the power of positivity to actually help yourself instead of holding yourself back?
• What truly makes us happy and how does that relate to success? Is it money? Social position? Friends, family? Health? **No. There's actually something bigger, deeper, and much more fundamental behind our happiness.** You will be surprised to find out what the factor that ultimately drives us and keeps us going is, and this discovery can greatly improve your life.
• **Why our Western perception of both happiness and success are fundamentally wrong,** and how those misperceptions can kill your chances of

succeeding?

• **Why relying on willpower and motivation is a very bad idea, and what to hold on to instead?** This is as important as using only the best gasoline in a top-grade sports car. Fill its engine with a moped fuel and keep the engine oil level low, and it won't get far. Your mind is this sports car engine. I will show you where to get this quality fuel from.

• **You will learn what the common denominator of the most successful and disciplined people on this planet is** – Navy SEALS and other special forces, Shaolin monks, top performing CEOs and Athletes, they, in fact, have a lot in common. I studied their lives for a long time, and now, it's time to share this knowledge with you.

• Why your entire life can be viewed as a piece of training, and **what are the rules of this training?**

• What the XX-th century Russian Nobel-Prize winner and long-forgotten genius Japanese psychotherapist **can teach you about the importance of your emotions and utilizing them correctly in your quest to becoming a self-disciplined and a peaceful person?**

• How modern science can help you **overcome temptation and empower your will**, and why following strict and inconvenient diets or regimens can actually help you achieve your goals in the end?

• How can you win by failing and **why giving up on some of your goals can actually be a good thing?**

• How do we often become **our own biggest enemies** in achieving our goals and how to finally change it?

• How to **maintain** your success once you achieve it?

Direct Buy Link to Amazon Kindle Store: **http://tinyurl.com/IanMentalToughness**

Paperback version on Createspace: http://tinyurl.com/IanMTPaperback

Communication Skills Training: A Practical Guide to Improving Your Social Intelligence, Presentation, Persuasion and Public Speaking

Do You Know How To Communicate With People Effectively, Avoid Conflicts and Get What You Want From Life?

...It's not only about what you say, but also about WHEN, WHY and HOW you say it.

Do The Things You Usually Say Help You, Or Maybe Hold You Back?

Have you ever considered **how many times you intuitively felt that maybe you lost something important or crucial, simply because you unwittingly said or did something, which put somebody off?** Maybe it was a misfortunate word, bad formulation, inappropriate joke, forgotten name, huge misinterpretation, awkward conversation or a strange tone of your voice?
Maybe you assumed that you knew exactly what a particular concept meant for another person and you stopped asking questions?

Maybe you could not listen carefully or could not stay silent for a moment? **How many times have you wanted to achieve something, negotiate better terms, or ask for a promotion and failed miserably?**

It's time to put that to an end with the help of this book.

Lack of communication skills is exactly what ruins most peoples' lives.
If you don't know how to communicate properly, you are going to have problems both in your intimate and family relationships.

You are going to be ineffective in work and business situations. It's going to be troublesome managing employees or getting what you want from your boss or your clients on a daily basis. Overall, **effective communication is like an engine oil which makes your life run smoothly, getting you wherever you want to be.** There are very few areas in life in which you can succeed in the long run without this crucial skill.

What Will You Learn With This Book?

-What Are The **Most Common Communication Obstacles** Between People And How To Avoid Them

-How To Express Anger And Avoid Conflicts

-What Are **The Most 8 Important Questions You Should Ask Yourself** If You Want To Be An Effective Communicator?

-5 Most Basic and Crucial Conversational Fixes

-How To Deal With Difficult and Toxic People

-Phrases to **Purge from Your Dictionary** (And What to Substitute Them With)

-The Subtle Art of **Giving and Receiving Feedback**

-Rapport, the **Art of Excellent Communication**

-How to Use Metaphors to **Communicate Better** And **Connect With People**

-What Metaprograms and Meta Models Are and How Exactly To Make Use of Them To **Become A Polished Communicator**

-How To Read Faces and **How to Effectively Predict Future Behaviors**

-How to Finally Start **Remembering Names**

-How to Have a Great Public Presentation

-How To Create Your Own **Unique Personality** in Business (and Everyday Life)

-Effective Networking

Direct link to Amazon Kindle Store:
https://tinyurl.com/IanCommSkillsKindle

The Science of Effective Communication: Improve Your Social Skills and Small Talk, Develop Charisma and Learn How to Talk to Anyone

Discover the powerful way to transform your relationships with friends, loved ones, and even co-workers, with proven strategies that you can put to work immediately on improving the way you communicate with anyone in any environment.

From climbing the career ladder to making new friends, making the most of social situations, and even finding that special someone, communication is the powerful tool at your disposal to help you achieve the success you truly deserve.

In The Science of Effective Communication, you'll learn how to develop and polish that tool so that no matter who you are, where you go, or what you do, you'll make an impact on everyone you meet for all the right reasons.

Discover the Secrets Used By the World's Most Effective Communicators

We all know that one person who positively lights up any room they walk into, who seem to get on with everyone they meet and who lead a blessed life as a result.

Yet here's something you may not know:

Those people aren't blessed with a skill that is off-limits to the rest of us.

You too can learn the very same techniques used by everyone from Tony Robbins to Evan Carmichael to that one guy in your office who everyone loves and put them to work in getting what you want - without bulldozing over everyone in your path.

Step-by-Step Instructions to Supercharge Your Social Confidence

The Science of Effective Communication is a fascinating, practical guide to making communication your true super power, packed with expert advice and easy-to-follow instructions on how to:

- Retrain your brain to develop powerful listening skills that will help you build better relationships with anyone and gain more value from your conversations.
- Make your voice more attractive to potential romantic partners.
- Mend broken relationships with family members, partners, and even work colleagues.
- Get your views heard by those in authority without being disrespectful.
- Thrive in any job interview and get that dream job.

Your Complete Manual for Building Better Relationships With Everyone You Meet

Bursting with actionable steps you can use IMMEDIATELY to transform the way you communicate, this compelling, highly effective book serves as your comprehensive guide to better communication, revealing exclusive tips to help you:

- Overcome 'Outsider Syndrome,' make friends, and flourish in any social situation
- Keep conversations flowing with anyone
- Make long-distance relationships not only work, but positively prosper
- Reap huge rewards from a digital detox

And much, much more.

Direct Buy Link to Amazon Kindle Store:
http://getbook.at/EffectiveCommunication

Paperback version on CreateSpace: http://getbook.at/EffectiveCommPaper

The Science of Interpersonal Relations: A Practical Guide to Building Healthy Relationships, Improving Your Soft Skills and Learning Effective Communication

From first dates and successful relationships to friends, colleagues, and new acquaintances, <u>unlock the hidden secrets to successful communication with anyone</u> and learn to flourish in any environment.

Guaranteed to change the way you think about relationships forever, <u>The Science of Interpersonal Relations</u> empowers you to identify those communication skills you need to work on and develop powerful techniques that will ensure your interpersonal relations thrive.

Your Complete Guide to Transforming Your Relationships

<u>The Science of Interpersonal Relations</u> is a book unlike any you've read before, not only in its approach to improving romantic relationships, but also on how to strengthen bonds and communicate better friends, family members, and even colleagues.

To really help you change your entire approach to communication, the book is split into two easy-to-read parts.

In part one, you'll change the way you think about the different relationships in your life and develop a whole new mindset that will lead you to healthy, positive, long-lasting relationships.

You'll discover:

• The real reason why so many relationships break down, and how to prevent yours from doing the same

• How to identify when you're being emotionally abused, and how to make it stop for good.

• Powerful solutions for dealing with negative people and protecting yourself against emotional vampires

• The secrets to successful assertiveness and the right way to say 'no' to anyone

• The links between personality styles and communication, and how to get the best out of any conversation with anyone.

In part two, you'll learn the tools and techniques you can put into action RIGHT NOW to start transforming your interpersonal relations for the better, including:

• Proven strategies for setting boundaries without hurting the other person

• The simple way for to help you meet your partner's real needs

• Effective techniques for identifying your partner's need for validation and providing it and much more.

Discover the Real Reason You Don't Have the Relationship You Want - And What to Do About It

●Single and struggling to find that 'perfect' someone?

●In a relationship that you suspect might be in serious trouble?

●Dating someone you're convinced is 'The One' but not sure how to take that relationship to the next level?

Then this is the one book you can't live without.

Whatever situation you're in, single, dating, or struggling to keep that long-term relationship alive, you'll find simple-yet-effective instructions on how to create positive connections with the people in your life, including:
●How to determine what you really want in a relationship - and the red flags to watch out for that tell you someone really isn't right for you.
●How to turn heated arguments into positive experiences that help you and your loved one become closer and happier as a couple.
●How to identify if you're in a codependent relationship - and what to do about it.
●How to have "The Talk" about the state of your relationship and approach the subject of turning casual dating into something more serious.

Direct Buy Link to Amazon Kindle Store:

http://getbook.at/Relations

Paperback version on Createspace:

Emotional Intelligence Training: A Practical Guide to Making Friends with Your Emotions and Raising Your EQ

Do you believe your life would be healthier, happier and even better, if you had more practical strategies to regulate your own emotions?

Most people agree with that.

Or, more importantly:

Do you believe you'd be healthier and happier if everyone who you live with had the strategies to regulate their emotions?

...Right?

The truth is not too many people actually realize what EQ is really all about and what causes its popularity to grow constantly.

Scientific research conducted by many American and European universities prove that the **"common" intelligence responses account for less than 20% of our life achievements and successes, while the other over 80% depends on emotional intelligence.** To put it roughly: **either you are emotionally intelligent, or you're doomed to mediocrity, at best.**

As opposed to the popular image, emotionally intelligent people are not the ones who react impulsively and spontaneously, or who act lively and fiery in all types of social environments.

Emotionally intelligent people are open to new experiences, can show feelings adequate to the situation, either good or bad, and find it easy to socialize with other people and establish new contacts. They handle stress well, say "no" easily, realistically assess the achievements of themselves or others and are not afraid of constructive criticism and taking calculated risks.

They are the people of success. Unfortunately, this perfect model of an emotionally intelligent person is extremely rare in our modern times.

Sadly, nowadays, **the amount of emotional problems in the world is increasing at an alarming rate.** We are getting richer, but less and less happy. Depression, suicide, relationship breakdowns, loneliness of choice, fear of closeness, addictions—this is clear evidence that we are getting increasingly worse when it comes to dealing with our emotions.

Emotional intelligence is a SKILL, and can be learned through constant practice and training, just like riding a bike or swimming!

This book is stuffed with lots of effective exercises, helpful info and practical ideas.

Every chapter covers different areas of emotional intelligence and shows you, **step by step**, what exactly you can do to **develop your EQ** and become the **better version of yourself**.

I will show you how freeing yourself from the domination of left-sided brain thinking can contribute to your inner transformation—**the emotional revolution that will help you redefine who you are and what you really want from life!**

In This Book I'll Show You:

• What Is Emotional Intelligence and What Does EQ Consist of?

• How to **Observe and Express** Your Emotions

• How to **Release Negative Emotions** and **Empower the Positive Ones**

• How to Deal with Your **Internal Dialogues**

• How to **Deal with the Past**

• **How to Forgive** Yourself and How to Forgive Others

• How to Free Yourself from **Other People's Opinions and Judgments**

• What Are "Submodalities" and How Exactly You Can Use Them to **Empower Yourself** and **Get Rid of Stress**

• The Nine Things You Need to **Stop Doing to Yourself**

• How to Examine Your Thoughts

• **Internal Conflicts** Troubleshooting Technique

• The Lost Art of Asking Yourself the Right Questions and **Discovering Your True Self!**

• How to Create Rich Visualizations

• LOTS of practical exercises from the mighty arsenal of psychology, family therapy, NLP etc.

• **And many, many more!**

Direct Buy Link to Amazon Kindle Store:
https://tinyurl.com/IanEQTrainingKindle

Paperback version on Createspace: https://tinyurl.com/ianEQpaperback

Accelerated Learning: The Most Effective Techniques: How to Learn Fast, Improve Memory, Save Your Time and Be Successful

Unleash the awesome power of your brain to achieve your true potential, learn anything, and enjoy greater success than you ever thought possible.

Packed with proven methods that help you significantly improve your memory and develop simple-yet-powerful learning methods, Accelerated Learning: The Most Effective Techniques is the only brain training manual you'll ever need to master new skills, become an expert in any subject, and achieve your goals, whatever they may be.

Easy Step-by-Step Instructions Anyone Can Use Immediately

•Student preparing for crucial exams?

•Parent looking to better understand, encourage, and support your child's learning?

•Career professional hoping to develop new skills to land that dream job?

Whoever you are and whatever your reason for wanting to improve your memory, Accelerated Learning: The Most Effective Techniques will show you exactly how to do it with simple, actionable tasks that you can use to help you:

•Destroy your misconceptions that learning is difficult - leaving you free to fairly pursue your biggest passions.

•Stop procrastinating forever, eliminate distractions entirely, and supercharge your focus, no matter what the task at hand.

•Cut the amount of time it takes you to study effectively and enjoy more time away from your textbooks.

•Give yourself the best chance of success by creating your own optimal learning environment.

Everything you'll learn in this book can be implemented immediately regardless of your academic background, age, or circumstances, so no matter who you are, you can start changing your life for the better RIGHT NOW.

Take control of your future with life-changing learning skills.

<u>Self-doubt is often one of the biggest barriers people face in realizing their full potential and enjoying true success.</u>

In <u>Accelerated Learning: The Most Effective Techniques</u>, you'll not only find out how to overcome that self-doubt, but also how to thrive in any learning environment with scientifically-proven tools and techniques.

<u>**You'll also discover:**</u>
•How to use an ancient Roman method for flawless memorization of long speeches and complex information

•The secret to never forgetting anyone's name ever again.

•The easy way to learn an entirely new language, no matter how complex.

•The reason why flashcards, mind maps, and mnemonic devices haven't worked for you in the past - and how to change that.

•The simple speed-reading techniques you can use to absorb information faster.

- How to cut the amount of time it takes you to study effectively and enjoy more time away from your textbooks.

- The truth about binaural beats and whether they can help you focus.

- How to effectively cram any exam (in case of emergencies!).

And much more!

Direct Buy Link to Amazon Kindle Store:

http://getbook.at/AcceleratedLearning

Paperback version on Createspace:

http://getbook.at/AcceleratedLearningPaperback

The Science of Self Talk: How to Increase Your Emotional Intelligence and Stop Getting in Your Own Way

We all speak to ourselves on a daily basis. Whether it's out loud or an internal (or infernal) commentary, we all practice self-talk and, how we speak to ourselves can have a significant effect on our emotions and subsequent actions.

Some people's self-talk is mostly about the future while, for others, it's an internal dialogue about the past. Some self-talk is positive and upbeat, while other self-talk is harsh, critical or defeatist.

Self-talk can focus on other people but, more often than not, it is about ourselves - and is often negative.

If you listen carefully, you'll notice that your inner conversation reflects thoughts and emotions. Self-talk isn't random. It exhibits patterns that repeat themselves. And everyone has their own characteristic self-talk that is uniquely theirs.

In The Science Of Self-Talk mindfulness expert, Ian Tuhovsky, explains how we can re-write the script when it comes to our internal communication. Through a series of simple exercises for use in daily life, you can understand your own self-talk in order to change the conversation.

Learn how you can listen to and understand your internal dialogue in order to change it.

Many of us practice negative self-talk by default - how many times have you called yourself an idiot or chastised yourself for not being good enough?

Negative self-talk is a harmful habit which can lead to anxiety, depression and helplessness and, yet, this is something that most of us do on a regular basis. For many people, this is learned behaviour whereby caution against boasting leads to self-criticism or self deprecation. For others, this is a natural reflection of the self and one that can slowly corrode self esteem.

This unique book covers:

- Constructive self-talk and dysfunctional self-talk - and knowing the difference.
- The impact of negative self-talk
- Learned helplessness
- Positive self-talk - challenge or threat?

- The Pareto Principle which says that, for many events, roughly 80% of the effects come from 20% of the causes.
- Creating the right circumstances for motivation
- Getting to know yourself
- Loving yourself - emotional intelligence
- Turning down the volume on your self-talk

In the past, people who engaged in negative self-talk or self-criticism were often labelled 'perfectionists', insinuating that it's actually a positive thing but it's so much more damaging than that.

Learning to identify our negative self-talk behaviour is the first step toward freeing us from its grip. With the right tools, we can change our internal dialogue, opening ourselves up to new opportunities, increased self-esteem and confidence.

More than just a self-help manual, The Science of Self-Talk is a Positive Psychology Coaching Series which explains the roots of self-talk, or, intrapersonal communication. The book explains that these are the thoughts that we 'hear' with the auditory part of our brain and which add a kind of commentary to our daily life.

Self talk is a little like turning on the director's commentary on a movie.

You can simply watch the movie or you can add in commentary about what's happening in it - this is, in a nutshell, what most of us do in our daily lives.

The Science Of Self Talk can help you to re-write the script of your movie and improve the way that you - and others - see yourself.

Direct link to Amazon Kindle Store: **mybook.to/IanSelfTalk**

Mindfulness: The Most Effective Techniques: Connect With Your Inner Self to Reach Your Goals Easily and Peacefully

Mindfulness is not about complicated and otherworldly woo-woo spiritual practices. It doesn't require you to be a part of any religion or a movement.

What mindfulness is about is living a good life (that's quite practical, right?), and this book is all about deepening your awareness, **getting to know yourself**, and developing attitudes and mental habits that will make you not only a successful and effective person in life, but a happy and wise one as well.

If you have ever wondered what the mysterious words "mindfulness" means and why would anyone bother, you have just found your (detailed) answer!

This book will provide you with actionable steps and valuable information, all in plain English, so all of your doubts will be soon gone.

In my experience, **nothing has proven as simple and yet effective and powerful as the daily practice of mindfulness.**

It has helped me become more decisive, disciplined, focused, calm, and just a happier person.

I can come as far as to say that mindfulness has transformed me into a success.

Now, it's your turn.
There's nothing to lose, and so much to win!

The payoff is nothing less than transforming your life into its true potential.

What you will learn from this book:

-What exactly does the word "mindfulness" mean, and why should it become an important word in your dictionary?

-How taking **as little as five minutes a day** to clear your mind might result in steering your life towards great success and becoming a much more fulfilled person? ...and **how the heck can you "clear your mind" exactly?**

-What are the **most interesting, effective, and not well-known mindfulness techniques for success** that I personally use to stay on the track and achieve my goals daily while feeling calm and relaxed?

-**Where to start** and how to slowly get into mindfulness to avoid unnecessary confusion?

-What are the **scientifically proven profits** of a daily mindfulness practice?

-**How to develop the so-called "Nonjudgmental Awareness"** to win with discouragement and negative thoughts, **stick to the practice** and keep becoming a more focused, calm, disciplined, and peaceful person on a daily basis?

-What are **the most common problems** experienced by practitioners of mindfulness and meditation, and how to overcome them?

-How to meditate and **just how easy** can it be?

-What are **the most common mistakes** people keep doing when trying to get into meditation and mindfulness? How to avoid them?

-**Real life tested steps** to apply mindfulness to everyday life to become happier and much more successful person?

-What is the relation between mindfulness and life success? How to use mindfulness to become much more effective in your life and achieve your goals much easier?

-**What to do in life** when just about everything seems to go wrong?

-How to become a **more patient and disciplined person**?

Stop existing and start living.
Start changing your life for the better today.

Amazon Kindle Store:

myBook.to/IanMindfulnessGuide

Paperback version on Createspace:

http://tinyurl.com/IanMindfulnessGuide

Buddhism: Beginner's Guide: Bring Peace and Happiness to Your Everyday Life

Buddhism is one of the most practical and simple belief systems on this planet, and it has greatly helped me on my way to become a better person in every aspect possible. In this book I will show you what happened and how it was.

No matter if you are totally green when it comes to Buddha's teachings or maybe you have already heard something about them—this book will help

you systematize your knowledge and will inspire you to learn more and to take steps to make your life positively better!

I invite you to take this beautiful journey into the graceful and meaningful world of Buddhism with me today!

Direct link to Amazon Kindle Store:
https://tinyurl.com/IanBuddhismGuide

Paperback version on Createspace:
http://tinyurl.com/ianbuddhismpaperback

About The Author

Hi! I'm Ian...

. . . and I am interested in life. I am in the study of having an awesome and passionate life, which I believe is within the reach of practically everyone. I'm not a mentor or a guru. I'm just a guy who always knew there was more than we are told. I managed to turn my life around from way below my expectations to a really satisfying one, and now I want to share this fascinating journey with you so that you can do it, too.

I was born and raised somewhere in Eastern Europe, where Polar Bears eat people on the streets, we munch on snow instead of ice cream and there's only vodka instead of tap water, but since I make a living out of several different businesses, I move to a new country every couple of months. I also work as an HR consultant for various European companies.

I love self-development, traveling, recording music and providing value by helping others. I passionately read and write about social psychology, sociology, NLP, meditation, mindfulness, eastern philosophy, emotional intelligence, time management, communication skills and all of the topics related to conscious self-development and being the most awesome version of yourself.

Breathe. Relax. Feel that you're alive and smile. And never hesitate to contact me!

Made in the USA
San Bernardino, CA
15 February 2020